SCHOOL DISCIPLINE

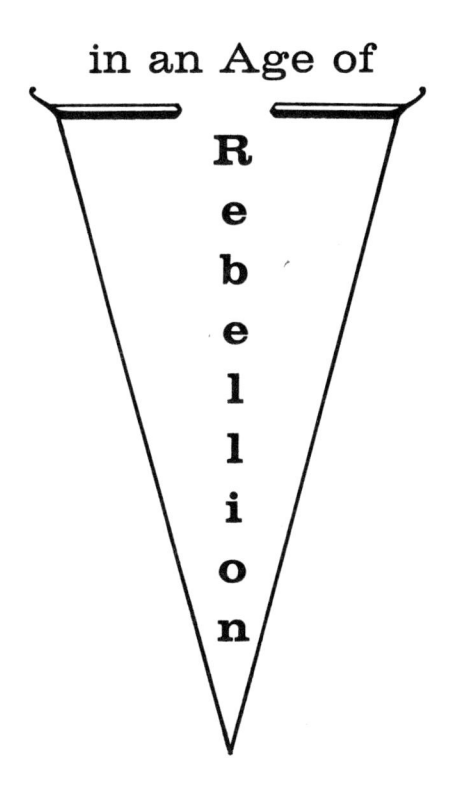

in an Age of

Rebellion

SCHOOL DISCIPLINE

in
an Age
of
Rebellion

Knute
Larson

Parker Publishing   **West Nyack,**
Company, Inc.   **New York**

© 1972, by

PARKER PUBLISHING COMPANY, INC.

West Nyack, N.Y.

All rights reserved. No part of this book may be reproduced in any form or by any means, without permission in writing from the publisher.

Library of Congress
Catalog Card Number: 75-182267

Printed in the United States of America
ISBN 0-13-792275-2
B & P

**This One Is For
KRIS ADRIAN LARSON**

Other Books by the Author:

Knute Larson and Melvin Karpas, *Effective Secondary School Discipline,* Prentice-Hall, Inc., 1963.

Knute Larson, *Guide to Personal Advancement in the Teaching Profession,* Parker Publishing Co., Inc., 1966.

Knute Larson and James McGoldrick, *Handbook of School Letters,* Parker Publishing Co., Inc., 1970.

Channeling the Actions and Aims of Today's Youth

As we proceeded into the seventies, a formidable youth rebellion started to move down from the colleges into our secondary schools. Already besieged by militant parents, militant taxpayers and teachers, and angry minority groups, some school administrators started to look for shelter from the storm.

Some sought avenues of retreat by changing from one job to another. Some surrendered to the strongest pressures while still going through the motions of doing their jobs. Some simply accepted the new challenges and began to convert the energies of rebellion into positive channels. It is the latter group that has inspired this book. Most of us are convinced there are good years ahead for American education after the tempest has abated. We shall have truly effective public schools throughout our land *if the American people do not lose their faith in public education.*

There have been, and will continue to be, times when extremists and fanatics seem to have educational leaders squeezed into the jaws of a vise. These extremists, having outshouted the moderates, seem to glory in the American pastime of proposing simple answers to complex problems. Instead of engaging in the compromises of serious political action, they scream slogans at each other.

"Law and Order" shout the bumper stickers; "Support Your Police;" "America—Love It or Leave It." These sentiments suggest we should somehow return to a halcyon past that never really existed. At the other end, we hear "Burn, Baby, Burn!";

"Make Love, Not War!"; "Kill the Pigs!"—strange slogans that demand a brave new world for which there is no blueprint.

We who work in the schools cannot escape from the youth rebellion any more than we can escape from other forms of militancy that have surfaced in recent years. There is no place to hide. We must, therefore, seek answers to central questions. *How can we work with militant groups to improve our schools? How can we help the youth "rebellion" to build a better nation?*

Basically, it is to these questions that this book is directed; to these and to the more specific issue of creating a better learning climate in our schools through a system of discipline that protects the rights of all in an honest atmosphere of justice, trust, and truth. Since many of us in the schools have learned from experience to mistrust simple solutions to difficult problems, we shall examine the elements of the youth rebellion, its slogans and stated issues, and, probing deeper, its hidden agenda, its real issues.

1. We shall examine the politics of confrontation, the "how to" of working effectively with militant groups, and the process of channeling the energies of anger into positive directions.

2. The drug problem will be reviewed with an emphasis on what schools can do in a community partnership to eliminate this terrifying threat to the young. Current court decisions centered around the rights of students will be examined and translated into procedural and policy patterns that help to establish authority without authoritarianism.

3. We shall examine the new problems of the classroom teacher and offer specific guidelines for effective teaching and learning today. Special consideration is given to the handling of severely alienated youth. Old methods have failed. New directions are suggested.

4. Since attitudes, especially teacher attitudes, are crucial to successful education today, practical recommendations are made for a human relations program for the school *and* its community. Schools can be islands no longer.

5. Attention is given to the improvement of curriculum and arrangements for learning. Finally, we review the major recommendations of the book in a format of specific action proposals.

The great majority of my colleagues knows that a small

minority of students causes a major portion of all discipline problems in our schools. It is still true that only a small minority is engaged in destructive activity. But there is a difference today. A majority of our students wants changes in our schools and communities. They want to contribute to effecting these changes, swiftly and legally. Often, however, they are captives of less positive mass actions which have been twisted into destructive results, ironically enough, by the manipulations of a willful minority. It is no longer a simple matter for the good school citizen to ignore the foolish acts of the bad school citizen. This is at the root of the frustrating problems facing educators today.

With cordial greetings to my colleagues who face with courage and wisdom the gathering storm—

Knute Larson

CONTENTS

Channeling the Actions and Aims of Today's Youth   7

1. ANATOMY OF A REVOLUTION **17**

   What Happened? — *20*

   > *The outside agitator theory*
   > *The generation war theory*
   > *The "liberalism has failed" theory*
   > *The man vs. machine theory*
   > *The participatory democracy theory*

   What Do They Want? — *23*
   Why Is This Youth Rebellion Different? — *24*

2. LIVING WITH MILITANCY IN OUR SCHOOLS **34**

   Student Militancy in Public Schools — *34*
   Where Did It Come From? — *35*

   > *Institutional differences*
   > *Differences in goals and expectations*
   > *Differences in recognition of adulthood*

   Why Our Secondary Schools? — *39*
   How Long Will It Last? — *40*
   What Are the Issues? — *41*
   What Forms Has Militancy Assumed? — *41*

   > *The rumble or riot*
   > *The boycott of classes*
   > *The strike and picketing*

The seizure of spaces
The slowdown
The underground press
Vandalism and sabotage

How Can We Contain Militancy and Channel It into Positive Directions? — 44
Planning Ahead for Trouble — 49

Introduction
Police liaison
Personnel orientation
Communications
Building security
Public information
Miscellaneous

3. COPING WITH THE NARCOTICS PROBLEM 53

Another American Dilemma — 54
The Marijuana Controversy — 55

What do we know?
What do scientists suspect?

Other Drugs in Common Use — 60

Narcotic drugs
Hallucinogens
Stimulant drugs (uppers)
Depressant drugs (downers)

An Action Program for Schools — 64
Recommended Program Elements — 66
The Role of the Teacher — 68

4. THE TEACHER WORKS WITH MILITANT YOUTH 69

It All Starts in the Classroom — 70

The sanctuary under attack
Student complaints
Implied complaints from our courts

Contents

The teacher's attitude

A Good Classroom Climate — 74

5. A CONTEMPORARY RATIONALE FOR
   SCHOOL DISCIPLINE **83**

   *American Democratic Tradition as a Base for
   Discipline* — 83
   Law as a Base for Discipline — 85

   *What happened to "in loco parentis"?
   The schools still have legal responsibilities
   Channeling student militancy*

   Humanitarian and Pragmatic Bases for Discipline — 88
   Authority Without Authoritarianism — 90

   *Freedom of expression
   The underground press
   Wearing buttons
   Acts of symbolism
   The compulsory flag salute
   Desecrating the flag
   Personal appearance
   Behavior codes
   Suspension and expulsion
   Corporal punishment*

6. MAINTAINING JUSTICE, LAW, AND
   ORDER IN THE SCHOOL **100**

   The Machinery of Justice — 100

   *Using teachers
   Using counselors
   Using department heads
   Using students*

   The Enforcement of Law — 107

   Working with the police

   The Maintenance of Law and Order — 110

   *Organization of personnel for emergencies
   Levels of preparedness*

7. WORKING WITH ALIENATED YOUTH . **115**

Getting Started — 117
To Segregate or Not to Segregate — 118

    The segregation of exceptional students

A Separate School — 120

    The Philadelphia advancement school

A School Within a School — 123

    The Chicago Ray school

A School Apart and Within — 124

    The Bristol Township opportunity school
    General recommendations for non-segregated treatment

8. HUMAN RELATIONS EDUCATION . . . **127**

Types of Human Relations Training — 128
By-Products of Human Relations Training — 129
Pitfalls to Avoid — 131

    Avoiding mistakes

Case History of a Training Program — 133
Postscript — 138

9. POLICIES AND REGULATIONS AFFECTING DISCIPLINE **140**

A Positive Approach — 142

    Proposed policy
    The flag salute ceremony

Sample Policies and Regulations — 146

    Constitutional guarantees to juveniles
    Policy 1411 and proposed administrative
      regulation 1411
    Discipline and punishment
    Drug and narcotics control
    Freedom of speech
    Disruption of school

Contents

10. **IMPROVING THE CLIMATE FOR LEARNING** **157**

    Needed–An Auxiliary Administrative Unit — *160*
    The Ordering of Goals — *162*
    The Emergence of Accountability Through Better Data Processing — *163*
    Organizing Our Schools — *165*

    > *The extended school year*
    > *The extended school day*

    Work-Experience Extensions — *169*
    Staffing Our Schools — *172*
    Innovation and Discipline — *174*

11. **ACTION REVIEW** **176**

    Evidence, Rationale, Action — *176*

    > *Is there a youth revolution?*
    > *Action*
    > *Militancy and discipline*
    > *Action*
    > *The deluge of drugs*
    > *Action*
    > *The payoff is the classroom*
    > *Action*
    > *A democratic and humanitarian base for discipline*
    > *Action*
    > *Justice, law, and order*
    > *Action*
    > *The problem of alienated youth*
    > *Action*
    > *Human relations training*
    > *Action*
    > *Policies and regulations*
    > *Action*
    > *Discipline and better arrangements for learning*
    > *Action*

Index **193**

1

> Revolutions do not occur because new ideas suddenly develop, but because a new generation begins to take old ideas seriously—not merely as interesting theoretical views, but as the basis for political action and social change.
>
> **Kenneth Keniston** [1]

Anatomy of a Revolution

One of the characteristics of an ailing society is the tendency to replace action with reaction. Changes are made only as responses to actions of another group. America's foreign policy since World War II, for example, has frequently consisted of responses; our agonizing appraisal of American education after the ascent of *Sputnik I* promised to become the most significant event in the history of American education. Now we are faced by another startling phenomenon in the form of the

---

[1] "You Have to Grow Up in Scarsdale to Know How Bad Things Really Are." Kenneth Keniston, *New York Times Magazine,* April 27, 1969.

most dramatic and positive actions, which could, if we act decisively and intelligently, help to revolutionize our schools and our society. That phenomenon is often referred to as *The Youth Revolution.*

Chaotic and formless, this worldwide movement of the sixties needs to be understood by all Americans. It *must* be understood by those of us who work with young people. We must look behind its sometimes ugly facade, through its seemingly negative image, to the solid and uncomplicated idealism which forms its foundation. We must ask searching questions and we cannot accept knee-jerk answers.

This is a book about school discipline. The behavior of children and youth in school is, of course, influenced by what goes on *in* school, but far more important influences exist *outside* of school. We must examine these influences if we hope to continue as effective educators. This book will examine some of them and will attempt to provide practical solutions to the problems of educators today, who are facing what will probably be the most difficult and challenging period in the entire lifespan of American education. Guidelines and prescriptions must be based on opinions. I intend to express my opinions. They shall be based primarily on direct experience, secondarily on research.

Many observers, at the time of this writing, seem to feel that the youth revolution has about run its course. They point to the disappearance from the press of stories about the leaders. Some of them seem to have been swallowed up by the Establishment. Some are serving time in prison. Violence, they correctly assert, cannot be sustained indefinitely. The movement, they tell us, has come in like a ninth wave from the sea, and has broken in a swirl of foam.

I do not intend to debate this position; however, in my opinion there is substantial evidence that the youth revolution has not dissipated but has changed in form. We simply cannot ignore the fact that many of its initial demands have been granted. Indeed, a portion of the revolution has already been institutionalized, particularly at the university level. In later chapters, I will attempt to show how these and other demands have been accepted by our courts and public schools. In a very objective way, we can point to significant successes for the movement.

Who can say what effect the revolt of our young has had on the seemingly endless war in Viet Nam? The war certainly seems to be on its way to some sort of whimpering conclusion. With its passing will go a substantial portion of the motivation for the youth revolution. Will the war's end finish this movement? I do not know. I do not think so. I agree with a 1969 statement of John D. Rockefeller, III to the press:

> . . . I do not believe that they will slip easily into the comforts of suburbia and the career, leaving behind their idealism and impulse for change.

In my opinion, the current youth revolution is unique, essentially wholesome, and not a transitory adventure that will dissipate if we ignore it. It has important and direct implications for all facets of our educational system, and most especially for that facet we choose to call discipline. As members of the Establishment being revolted against, we only have two legitimate courses of action:

1. We can crush the revolution with increasing applications of force. We control the hardware of destruction.
2. We can learn to understand the revolution, seek out its positive aspects, and guide it into constructive channels.

At its foundation, the youth rebellion of the sixties in America has been part of a worldwide movement to restore the dignity of the individual and make the institutions of society more responsive to the needs of man. We have long been accustomed to the demonstrations and violence created by students in nations with unstable governments. Now we are beginning to see the almost foolhardy protests of young people in Iron Curtain countries where the governments appear to be very stable and very oppressive. (There the government blames outside agitators who are the tools of Washington.) We are also seeing something which puzzles us—the revolt of students in prosperous western nations where most people enjoy full stomachs and democratic rights. Most confusing of all, we see in our own nation a massive revolt of our own youth, often led by youngsters who enjoy enormous privileges and directed against universities with the most liberal reputations! (Here many elders blame outside agitators who are the tools of Moscow.)

Why is this happening? What is going on? Where have we (who like to think we have given these kids everything), failed?

WHAT HAPPENED?

The Bible teaches us that everything has a season. History teaches us the overwhelming power of an idea that is in season. In 1928, Norman Thomas ran for President on a platform of many ideas that were not in season. Their time eventually came, and now many of these ideas are accepted by both major political parties.

Student radicals have always been with us but their ideas have generally not been in season. In the fifties the college student was pictured with justification as a conformist, one who had everything and could look forward to selecting a good job from a veritable employment smorgåsbord. But all of the injustices of the world in the sixties were very much with the students of the fifties. With the possible exceptions of serious overpopulation and the pollution of our environment, they were *worse* in the fifties than they were a decade later. Today's students would say that their older brothers "copped out." Most young people took little or no group action to change their world. Those who were deeply concerned turned inwardly to become beatniks and sought escape in colorful and obscure religions and philosophies. They formed a "beatified" generation that acknowledged a lack of power to change society and simply withdrew from the mainstream of life to preserve their values.

The end of the decade of the fifties coincided with the beginning of a new season for the idealism of youth. With the Kennedy administration came a surge of hope for young people. From the accelerating militancy of American blacks and from student rebellions in other countries came the start of lessons in strategy. The possibility that real changes would take place and the dazzling successes of pressure and confrontation techniques began to intoxicate imaginative youngsters. Leadership popped

Anatomy of a Revolution 21

to the surface. Sometimes it involved the mere grabbing of a microphone at the right time. The right time was usually when TV or news cameras were focused on the right position.

Young Americans had exciting opportunities to express themselves in the sixties—civil rights marches and sit-ins, campus revolts, political rallies. The experiences were exhilarating, but also frustrating. Militancy spread rapidly as the students in more obscure colleges and junior colleges watched the exciting scenes at Berkeley and other centers of radical action on the 11 o'clock television news. Everybody wanted to "get into the act." Almost everybody did, sooner or later.

Dramatic and tragic events served to polarize American youth and toughen their idealism with a touch of cynicism— the assassination of three great men whom they admired; the failure of the McCarthy campaign; and the brutal events at the Pentagon and in Chicago. These experiences added a dimension of reality to the youth revolution which, in the long run, gave it greater staying power.

At this point, however, the movement began to drown in a sea of rhetoric. College students and young professors talk well. They began to talk—and talk and talk and talk. Amendments to amendments to resolutions were debated endlessly. Six-hour meetings would end with no agreements. Candid observers have indicated over and over again that many campus movements in this period literally talked themselves to death.

Many theories have been advanced as to the origins of the youth rebellion. Let us very briefly examine a few:

1. *The Outside Agitator Theory* assumes that a small minority of professional radicals is responsible for all of the acts of rebellion and defiance. The majority goes along with them mostly to be entertained.

   It has become perfectly clear that some groups do exist whose avowed procedures include violence and destruction. Perhaps the most dramatic of these is the *Weathermen,* a splinter group of the SDS (Students for a Democratic Society).

   Aware of the failure of the SDS to work with American blacks or to have the slightest influence on American labor, this group became disgusted with the constant talk in SDS and sought action. Completely ignoring the successes of SDS in achieving campus reform, notably at Columbia, they concluded that most SDS students failed to take the movement seriously. This is a dangerous faction which openly states that American society must be destroyed before it can be rebuilt. This type of action cannot be tolerated.

2. *The Generation War Theory* assumes that it is perfectly normal for the young to hate their elders and want to shock them. This rebellion is merely an action of this type by kids who have too much money, too much time, too much of everything.

3. *The Liberalism Has Failed Theory* acknowledges that the liberalism born in the French and American Revolutions may have achieved some success but that it is a failure today. The young feel that this liberalism died with the New Deal in Chicago in 1968. Now they want to replace it but they have yet to agree upon a design.

4. *The Man vs. Machine Theory* is based on the too-rapid advance of technology as opposed to the too-slow development of human relations skills. A computer society dehumanizes man. The young want to retain their individuality and so they are fighting against the machine.

5. *The Participatory Democracy Theory* assumes that the young reject the format of our republic because too much of the power is in the hands of too few. They point out that 80% of the wealth is controlled by 20% of the people, and wealth means power. All citizens should share in a direct way in choices which affect their lives. A direct way is, presumably, the confrontation technique where power groups face each other. Berkeley students can often be heard chanting "Power to the people. Who are the people? We are the people."

There are, of course, many other theories. Some of them are brilliant. Some of them are silly. Each seems to contain at least a seed of truth. We in education have little time for theorizing. Can we not proceed with three simple assumptions?

1. We have taught students well about freedom, justice, and equality. They took us seriously.

2. We failed to teach them that we didn't always mean what we said. They have recognized our hypocrisy but have failed to adopt it as a way of life.

3. The season has come (and, some say, has passed) for

their revolt. We must learn to use it for badly needed reforms.

WHAT DO THEY WANT?

Before we examine the situation at the secondary school level, we should remember the tendency of high school students to imitate college students. Although there is a noticeable commonness in militant youth movements all over the world, America's version differs in some ways. Only in America is the racial problem a significant factor in the youth rebellion. Only in America is the drug problem truly formidable. Only in America has the idea that almost everyone should go to college had such universal appeal.

The American tradition of upward social mobility has almost created a situation of disgrace for the young person who wants to become a skilled worker and who is completely satisfied with his social status. When pressures drive him into college, he becomes frustrated. This is especially true if he attends a weak academic college and knows in his heart that he is wasting time.

I feel that, briefly stated, many young Americans are seeking a true participatory democracy, with justice and equal opportunity for all. They know that before they became militant nobody over 30 paid much attention to them.

In their colleges many professors seemed more interested in research and writing than in teaching. The more eminent a professor became, the fewer students he taught.

Their universities seemed indifferent to the community around them. Slum housing was being torn down to make room for gyms and offices. Poor people were made homeless to provide room for more institutional bigness.

They felt that their country was waging an unjust war, and they did not want to die for a cause they seriously questioned.

They believed that minority groups had not yet been given true freedom.

They felt powerless, left out of the mainstream of history.

They felt that their elders were hypocrites who exploited the young.

The unfortunate fact is that although some of these beliefs

are overstated and some are half-truths, there is truth in all of them. Any one of them, compounded by some act of an institution, could be used by a cadre of activists to promote a demonstration. There never seems to be a shortage of issues. A demonstration plus a tactical administrative error plus a touch of brutality in suppression, equals a full-scale riot. Radical leaders know this and exploit it to the hilt. But they also know that they cannot sustain tension indefinitely. A majority of students are seriously concerned with getting an education. The issues selected had better make sense to a large number of intelligent youngsters.

The one issue that seems to stand out as a unifying force with any student body is harsh suppression and, especially, brutality through the use of physical force. It is quite possible that this is a major reason for the long-sustained state of semi-permanent warfare at Berkeley and San Francisco State. There the relationships between students and the Establishment resemble conditions in the Middle East. College administrators are facing terribly difficult decisions today. Public school administrators have also faced them, the most delicate decision of all being the precise moment when police assistance is necessary. If help is called too early, the resultant backlash may (and has) caused senseless killing. If help is called too late, the same tragic consequences may result. Someone must make a decision. That is the real dilemma of top school administration today.

WHY IS THIS YOUTH REBELLION DIFFERENT?

In my opinion, today's youth worker who faces the high school version of the campus revolution must accept two unpleasant facts: (1) this is not a new and transitory phenomenon, but a ten-year-old, worldwide movement that is beginning to mature and harden into permanence; (2) this is not simply a large-scale version of the perennial outbursts of youth. It is not a mammoth panty raid. The youth revolution of the sixties differs from any previous youth movements in several significant ways:

   1. *The Youth Rebellion Is Formless and Is Not Yet Dominated by Any Single Ideology.*

A close examination of each American campus revolt will reveal that tremendous efforts have been made by groups such as SDS, Progressive Labor (Maoist), The Young Socialist Alliance (Trotskyite), W.E.B. Dubois Clubs (Kremlin Communist), and many others organized around central issues (e.g. The National Committee to Abolish the House Un-American Activities Committee), to impose a unifying ideology on the youth revolution. To date, these efforts have failed. Although the youth rebellion is basically radical in that it wants to make sweeping changes in a hurry, it does not have a right wing and a left wing. But these groups like to think of themselves as *The New Left* and *The New Right*.

SDS, the largest single group within the youth revolution, provides a convenient umbrella when a campus becomes solidified behind an issue or issues. The order of events usually follows a familiar pattern: (a) A group of student activists (usually a small one to start) decides to rally around a cause that can be anything from campus R.O.T.C. to permitting women in men's dorms. (b) A demonstration is publicized by leaflets, etc. If the weather is good and the place selected is convenient to all, a fairly large crowd will turn out to see the action. (c) Police officers are goaded into action by the insults of activists and someone is arrested. The arrestee forces the officer to use force. (d) More police are called and a riot begins to take shape. (e) Mass arrests are made, with photographers snapping pictures and probably one or more television trucks moving into position. On more than one occasion, these gentlemen of the press have been known to *stage* dramatic events when things got dull! (f) An entire campus is now polarized around a gut issue, police brutality. (g) Large numbers of students turn to SDS as a focal spot because SDS has a rented facility that includes a telephone, a typewriter, and a duplicating machine. (h) The issue is finally resolved in one way or another and the students no longer need the SDS umbrella. It is returned to the closet until another rainy day.

2. *The Youth Rebellion Has Failed to Define Its Goals.*

The liberal movement in America has achieved many of its goals that were identified in the thirties. We know that we can produce more goods and services than people can use. We have failed to find an equitable way to distribute these goods and services to eliminate poverty in the midst of plenty. Many of the leaders of the youth rebellion have had all of the *things* they need. They do not see poverty as a necessary evil. To them society *must* abolish poverty *now*. The welfare client, in their eyes, should not be forced to request more aid. He should demand it because it is his right as a citizen. We should note that student positions vis-a-vis administrators seldom include *requests*. At the least they are called *demands*. Often they are termed *non-negotiable* demands.

In real negotiations, of course, there is no such demand. This new and frightening dimension in human relations is like a game of social Russian roulette. If the not negotiable demand is unreasonable, violence is nearly inevitable.

As indicated earlier, the student movement has, to date, rejected any single, enveloping ideology. The young rebels are impatient. They know what they are against, but they have yet to agree on exactly what they are for. It is precisely in this area that the elders can make a contribution. It must be made carefully because young people are very wary of being "co-opted" by the Establishment. The young have demonstrated their power to create change. It is now up to someone in authority to channel that power.

3. *The Youth Rebellion Rejects or Is Ignorant of the Lessons of History.*

History seems to have become irrelevant, if not to individual analysis at least to the formulation of group positions. Individual students may be studying for Ph.D. degrees in history, but when they become part of a group they seem to act as if the present exists in a vacuum. They seem to feel that no police action is justified when a mob breaks the law if the mob has a just cause. Who can doubt that the gang of hoodlums who gathered in a Munich beerhall some 40 years ago thought they had a just cause? Who can help but wonder if prompt and effective police action in that particular riot might possibly have saved the lives of millions of people?

Any member of the present middle-aged generation knows that he has had vast experiential advantages over young people today. One can hardly dispute the brutal maturing reality of the Depression of the thirties and of World War II. Millions of young people of that era were thrust into positions of great responsibility at a very early age. Those who survived became seasoned adults quite early in life. Young people from suburbia who go to college today face a serious handicap in maturing early but having real mature responsibilities postponed for a long time.

There are, of course, dramatic exceptions to this. People who grow up in our ghettos seem to move from infancy to hardened maturity without enjoying any significant childhood. Many of our young, of course, do experience war. In our system (at least up to the draft reforms of 1970), those who were fortunate enough to be able to attend college had this experience deferred or eliminated. Many young people have found these necessary maturing experiences in the Peace Corps, VISTA, or other forms of service. Most of them are finding these experiences by being deeply involved in the youth revolution.

Young people today seem to feel that the lessons of the thirties and forties are irrelevant now. (I often wish they would invent a relevant synonym for irrelevant, as well as a new set of curse words, which they have borrowed from older generations.)

Even among the under-30 group, there is evidence that subdivisions of the generation gap exist. It is not merely a struggle between the old and the young. A pronounced gap is appearing between the very young and the relatively young. Confusing? You bet it is.

I have observed a college student of 21 discussing the Eugene McCarthy presidential campaign to an audience that included a handful of high school students in their upper teens. During the discussion period, sharp questions were raised by the high school students. In a short period of time it became clear that they rejected the analyses of the older student and that they considered the lessons of the sixties as irrelevant as the lessons of the thirties!

This attitude about the past contributes immensely to the communications gap between the old and the young. When the experiences of the old are rejected by the young, who speak of "quality of experience" being more important than "quantity of experience," there isn't really much left to talk about. When anyone over 30 says "When I was your age . . ." to anyone under 30, chances are communications stop right then and there.

A major reason for this difficulty to understand the impatience of youth with the lessons of history is probably rooted in the sober fact that lasting reforms come slowly. It is also disheartening for the young to analyze the aftermaths of important revolutions in history. They want to shut their eyes and ears to the voices of the past. Their revolution is different they feel. As in their first experiences with love, their hearts tell them that nothing quite like this has ever happened before. Perhaps if we elders could try to remember our own youth on occasion, we might be able to understand this delightful phenomenon.

4. *The Youth Revolution Includes Several Equal but Separate Revolutions.*

In the early stages of the Black Civil Rights movement of the fifties, whites marched with blacks as brothers and, on many occasions, went to jail with them. Integration was central to the cause. The end of the sixties saw the integration movement still passing slowly through the courts into the schools. Until 1970, sections of our nation were permitted to delay school integration by various tactics. It was ironic that at this time it became clear that the more militant blacks no longer seemed to care about integration. They began to espouse a kind of equal apartheid that sounded curiously like the old "separate but equal" concept of public education in the South. The difference lay, of course, in the interpretation of the word *equal.*

Black extremists have clearly rejected white liberals as comrades in a single cause. They seem to feel that the white liberal's paternalism and tendency to take over cannot be tolerated. "This is our thing," they say, "Don't you try to take it over." In New York City in 1969 at the City University of New York, the black revolution ran a collision course with the youth revolution, as represented by a substantial percentage of Jewish liberal students. Racism is not less ugly when it comes from those who have been its victim. At the time of this writing, there is little reason to hope for less ugliness in our largest city.

The best evidence of the divisive mood of the militant black leadership is found in certain northern liberal colleges which have been predominantly white. These institutions were well known for their sincere efforts to attract black students and black teachers for several years. As these young blacks entered, they were carefully integrated into housing and all other aspects of school life.

College administrators were shocked when these students revolted (in one case they were actually armed) and demanded apartheid. They wanted their own housing, they wanted to eat together, and they wanted a department of black studies with black instructors. This is a growing pattern which I feel will do more harm than good for both blacks and whites. Moderate black leaders are particularly contemptuous of the proliferation of black studies. At the college level, they feel, the black student has no identity problem. What he needs is preparation for earning a superior station in life. In spite of the merits of this argument, the students seem to feel that they need each other more than they need integration. This pattern of protest will probably sweep the country, and undoubtedly some manifestations of it will filter down to the secondary schools.

Not the least damaging effect of the collegiate apartheid will be in the inherent weakness of any instantly created departments of studies. At their worst, they will be empty of scholarship and full of propaganda compounded out of wishful thinking and half-baked ideas. At best, they will be unneeded reinforcements of racial pride which the black students already have at that stage of their lives. Ironically, many of these unsubstantial academic experiences will take place in first-class institutions where black students have an enormous opportunity to prepare for badly needed leadership in tomorrow's world. The real value of a good black studies program will accrue to white students!

The misguided efforts of some militant blacks have forced a polarization within the young black community. It is very difficult to choose a position when only two alternatives are presented: being a militant or being an Uncle Tom. It is easy for a white youngster in an average community to select one of any number of positions in regard to militancy. He can always find a like-minded peer group. The black youngster is more often subjected to segregated housing. Thus he is forced into daily confrontation with militants. Unlike the white student, he cannot avoid them. Thus he may grow an afro haircut and mouth militant slogans as a means of survival.

It is very important for the teachers and administrators in a biracial school to understand this, particularly if they function in a community where the blacks are in a minority and live in segregated housing. Platitudes about independent thinking are falling on deaf ears in cases like this. The independent thought may be there, but it is hidden by a facade that is more acceptable to the group that holds the physical power.

Another factor in the black segment of the youth rebellion that must be understood by the white educator is the growing importance of a very basic human emotion—a desire for vengeance. "An eye for an eye, and a tooth for a tooth" is as old as the primitive concept of a vengeful deity in the early Hebrew religion. A god of vengeance appears in almost every ancient religion. It is an omnipresent motivation in man. Can we not understand that *black revenge* has appeared as a basic issue?

Once accepted, this fact is small comfort to the bewildered white administrator. If a demonstration is directed at specific issues, he has choices to make. If it is an act of revenge, he has but one choice—to restore order in any way he can. This is the cold and cruel fact of life every school administrator must face. His only judgment decision can be to define the delicate point where genuine issues stop and simple revenge begins. Here is a situation where the principal really earns his pay. The only guideline I can offer is a reminder that no professional principal really needs—that the safety and welfare of *all* his students must take precedent over the actions of a few.

Similar trends, similar polarization of radicals and moderates, similar frustrations and motivations may be found in many other identifiable American groups. Puerto Ricans see their problems as unique. Our Cuban guests see theirs as unique. Mexican-Americans have many legitimate complaints. Young Indians are deeply troubled by the complex problems of their people. All of these multi-faceted problems are reflected in our schools, and a school is one institution of our society that cannot afford to ignore its problems.

Puerto-Rican Americans come closest to having common cause with the black revolution because of their physical locations in the common ghettos of our major cities. The Harlem Puerto Rican has many problems in common with the Harlem black, but there are also significant differences between the two groups. The Puerto Rican has a homeland, he has a language, he has a culture of his own. The American black has had these things taken away from him over a period of three centuries. This makes his needs truly unique.

The only significant common bond among young revolutionaries of all groups seems to be that all of them disagree with the elders of their own group. They also share a vitriolic contempt for members of their own group of any age who are moderate or who curry favor with a more dominant group. One must almost go back to the Irish Revolution of 1916 and consider the attitude of an IRA activist to an Irish informer to find a parallel with the attitude of a black militant toward an "Uncle Tom" or that of an activist Mexican-American toward a "Tio Taco" (Uncle Hamburger).

All of these things complicate the work of the educator. More than one administrator, for example, has made the mistake of assuming that *any* black teacher can help to solve a racial problem involving blacks and whites.

5. *Today's Young Revolutionaries Will Not Necessarily Shift Their Views Significantly and in Large Numbers as They Grow Older.*

Many people who hold radical views in college soften in their attitudes as they grow older. Many continue to hold these views but never mention them except at cocktail parties after a fifth martini. There is something about facing the "realities of life" that is supposed to take the edge off a radical. Evidence is beginning to accumulate that this generation of radicals will probably be different, however.

Consider the 1969 revolt of soldiers in an Army stockade. Regardless of the merit or the lack of merit of their cause, these young men were certainly facing the realities of life. Carrying on a revolt in an Army stockade is not considered to be a healthy pursuit. The men who did it must have been convinced that they were right. Consider an even more bizarre type of revolt carried on by a group of soldiers under fire who had refused to move on to further battle because they were weary or because they were not convinced of the logic of the move. Consider the fact reported by many observers that for the first time in our history experienced leaders feel it necessary to convince their men of the logic of almost any move made in battle zones.

Consider the general attitude of young soldiers today as expressed in their songs, their underground newspapers, their hair style, etc. Consider the photograph in *National* magazine of a young army lieutenant with a peace sign painted on his helmet and a flower decal on his rifle. If the Army cannot contain the youth revolution in a battle area or in a stockade, we had better not underestimate the resolve of this generation.

An increasing number of young professionals refuse to work for firms which deal in military hardware or even firms which serve no readily identifiable purpose connected with the welfare of people. These young people turn to ghetto clinics, storefront law firms, public projects where they can do the most good for the people who need the most help. Perhaps it is too early to tell, but these are hardly signs of a generation that will "cop out" when it moves into suburbia.

Mr. Louis Harris of the public opinion firm bearing his name spoke of this question before a group of educators and students at Harvard in the summer of 1969. His firm is convinced that this youth group will substantially remain in what he calls a "change coalition," and that sampling techniques were changed to include people over 16 instead of cutting it off at 21. Mr. Harris also believes that this youth group will tip the balance between the "change coalition" and the "no change coalition" by the mid-seventies.

At the moment of this writing, a copy of *The Falmouth Enterprise* [2] (Cape Cod, Massachusetts) has been placed before me. On the front page is a photograph of a young man of 22 who is running for selectman. Two youthful campaign managers stand beside him. One of them is quoted in the accompanying article:

> We feel that Woods Hole needs a more effective voice in the town. . . . We feel no more motels should be allowed in the town. . . . We would like to see a training program sponsored by the town to train young people in the fishing industry. We feel that public housing should be enlarged and a town mental health clinic created.

This young man may not be elected this time but he and others like him will have their season. I feel that when that time comes, they will still want clinics and public housing rather than motels. We have urged them to work within our system, and that seems to be precisely what many of them will do. Perhaps they will tolerate more time for change, but change will come. Every tick of the clock brings it nearer to realization.

Some implications are clear for educators. Those who work with young people must make greater efforts to *really listen* to them, to accord their opinions genuine respect. They need our help whether they like to admit it or not. Before we can help them, we must understand (not necessarily accept) what they feel has happened to them, why it happened, and how we can begin to accommodate them in our existing institutions without endless angry confrontations.

The secret of this accommodation must be in change. *They* must change. *We* must change. Most of all our institutions must

---

[2] *The Falmouth Enterprise,* Falmouth, Massachusetts, January 15, 1971.

Anatomy of a Revolution 33

change. We must give up our deeply ingrained defense mechanisms that are so typical of educators. Is our record of achievement really so good that we can defend everything we are doing in our schools? I think not. Great changes are needed, and I feel that responsible students can help us in making these changes.

Teachers have also become militant in recent years. Professional negotiations have brought unprecedented gains for teachers, in working conditions and salaries. The keynote of effective negotiations is that each side approaches the table *in good faith*. The teachers expect the school board to meet with them in good faith. Is it unreasonable that they be expected to communicate with their students in good faith when there is a gap between opinions?

Clashes have already occurred between teacher militancy and student militancy. Especially in ghetto schools, students have questioned the quality of instruction and have been extremely impatient with interpretations of tenure laws. Teacher reaction has been largely defensive, denying that ineffective teaching takes place. Unfortunately, the record shows that too little learning takes place in these schools. Parents and students are blaming teachers. Teachers are blaming parents and students. Perhaps they are both right. Ineffective teaching usually reflects poor training and a lack of good in-service education. Neither of these factors can be blamed on the teacher who is unprepared to teach in a ghetto school.

A more dramatic clash, however, is taking place in the area of discipline. Students are demanding less oppression and more recognition of individual rights. Teachers are demanding (sometimes in their contracts) more oppressive disciplinary control and punishment. Perhaps they are both right. Stricter treatment of willful offenders does not necessarily require more oppressive treatment for non-offenders.

Let us move along the educational spectrum to the secondary schools and even to the upper elementary grades, where the youth revolution is moving swiftly onto the scene. Let us consider some guidelines for working with youngsters who will be different from anything we have yet encountered.

2

> Save us from weak resignation to
> the evils we deplore . . .
>
> Harry Emerson Fosdick [1]

Living with Militancy in Our Schools

STUDENT MILITANCY IN PUBLIC SCHOOLS

Public school educators have long been concerned with the varied and perplexing problems of discipline. Until the concluding years of the sixties, however, such problems usually involved individuals or small groups of students in situations which happened without advance planning or warning. Today these problems are still very much with us, but a new dimension has been added in the form of planned pressure tactics

---

[1] Harry Emerson Fosdick, *God of Grace and God of Glory,* Presbyterian Hymnal.

Living with Militancy in Our Schools

involving much larger groups. These tactics vary from mild petitions of complaint to extreme violence and destruction of property. And they are not limited to "difficult" urban settings.

A much quoted study of February 1969, conducted by Jane Hunt and J. Lloyd Trump, under the auspices of the National Association of Secondary School Principals, queried every fifteenth high school principal in America including the heads of private and parochial schools.

In the rapid developments of our times, this excellent report will quickly become obsolete and other studies will replace it. Three quotations from this historic document will suffice:

> The message is clear. Student activism is here. Three out of five principals report some form of active protest in their schools. Many who note no protest as yet add that they expect it in the near future.

Two unidentified principals wrote:

> To be a principal in times like these is not for the faint-hearted—and we're just getting started on this protest business.
>
> The students, to our utter despair, are exhibiting —at long last—the very kinds of behavior that we want to encourage, nourish, and develop as responsible educators. The requirements for (and agonies of) change are on our doorstep more so than on theirs. We must change or foster total revolution in our schools— public *or* private.

WHERE DID IT COME FROM?

The outside agitator theory is extremely popular in America. Often it has some basis in truth. More often it obscures the truth and leads us to disastrous courses of action. One thing seems clear today: *The problem differs significantly from the discipline problems of yesterday and requires different preventive and corrective measures.* A simple acceleration of force will not work unless we are prepared to go all the way and confront students with loaded guns. At one time I would have considered this unthinkable in America. Now we have the lessons of Kent State, Jackson State, and others to consider.

Because the more radical college movements have openly indicated their intentions to infiltrate the secondary schools, it was assumed early in the seventies that the college rebellion would simply move down into the secondary schools without significant change. There are many reasons for a substantial rejection of this theory, even though it fits the popular "outside agitator" theory of civil disobedience.

We must remember that the SDS and other college organizations also openly indicated an intention to find common cause with American labor. Instead they found almost total rejection and even violent opposition from American labor. The situation in our secondary schools is quite different from that of the colleges. There is also a very noticeable generation gap between the high school student and his older brother in college.

While it is perfectly clear that militancy and even radicalism is moving into our public schools, it is not at all clear that direction will be accepted from the college campus. We know, of course, that many high school students have and will continue to imitate what the mass media tells them is going on in colleges (especially underground newspapers which they cheerfully imitate). On the other hand, if these leaders expect to gain substantial support from their peers, they will have to take into account some significant differences. Let us consider a few of the more obvious differences:

1. *Institutional Differences.*

    Many issues in recent years have been generated out of educational institutions themselves, out of their seemingly irresponsive administrative structures, out of their alleged lack of concern for the student as an individual. Although it would be easy to identify common basic issues (such as the freedom of choices permitted to students), it is more important, in my opinion, to identify the truly significant differences between a college and a secondary school. For the most part, they seem obvious, but we must think of them in terms of their relationship to student protest in order to understand fully the current behavior of student activists at the two levels.

    Secondary school students are, of course, concerned with national and global issues. But it is difficult, in their case, to place much blame for these problems on their institution, on their teachers or administrators. Secondary school laboratories do not conduct research for the Pentagon or for war-related industries. Secondary teachers are not involved in research which alienates students. Secondary administrators, beyond their roles as citizens, do not have much to say about ending wars.

Occasionally, in our cities, a high school issue may parallel a university issue. When, for example, a new school must be built to serve a ghetto area, often homes and apartments must be condemned in order to create space for the new building. This happens when city universities require expansion. A dramatic example in recent years was the Columbia University gymnasium which was to be built on the edge of Harlem. Even though the University projected plans for Harlem residents to use the gym, the condemnation of housing units became a burning issue.

Apart from this type of problem, the secondary student's gut issues are derived from his experiences in his school. The personal freedoms of college students and high school students vary enormously. Freedom of choice is severely limited in the average high school, which is intended to serve *all* youth in a given age category who would not better be served by another type of institution. Seemingly oppressive regulations often are created out of a necessary concern for the safety of the entire student body. The storefront lawyer who scoffs at the repressive discipline of a city high school should be invited to teach in such a school for a week or two.

All of this does not, of course, make it easier for the conscientious student who must abide by petty regulations intended to contain the willful abuses of the lunatic fringe. He is concerned with *his* freedom of choice, the quality of the teaching to which *he* is exposed, and the relevance of the school curriculum to the life *he* will lead. Today's secondary administrator is deeply concerned with finding a way to grant greater freedom to those who are able to handle it, without interfering with the process of education or the rights of others.

2. *Differences in Goals and Expectations.*

College students still represent a select minority. Secondary students in public schools represent a cross-cut of the entire community. The liberal youth can easily espouse a hard line of anti-militarism. Many high school youngsters, on the other hand, regard the armed forces as their only opportunities to learn skills, to assume adult responsibilities, and to earn a living.

Most college students, each in his own way, seek a good way of life. For most of them, this includes an aspiration for above-average earnings. Many high school students look forward realistically to a lifetime of low earnings. Their goals are more immediate—a car, a television set—and their tolerance for delayed gratification is low because there is no promise of better days ahead. Their cynicism differs from that of the college students because their expectations are lower. Most of them are far more likely to demonstrate for a smoking area than for curriculum reform. Outside of directly job related learning experiences, many high school students regard the entire academic curriculum as a complete waste of time. The terrible truth is that they are sometimes at least partially right!

If the recent evidence of a sort of hard-hat counter-revolution reveals anything, it is that many of America's blue collar workers are moving toward the right, not the left of our political spectrum. In my opinion, a significant portion of that hard-line conservatism will come from the high school youngsters *who do not go on to further education* unless a depression and prolonged massive unemployment changes the picture. In that case, violent revolution may come—from the right *or* from the left.

The educator today who sees only incipient communism in student activism merely sees part of the picture. There is obvious incipient fascism in some youth activism. Intolerance of any but a "correct" viewpoint, destruction of property, and violence against persons have not been a monopoly of the left. Fanaticism abounds on both ends of the scale. America's working class has never exhibited much enthusiasm for the far left. Tomorrow's blue collar workers may find themselves tempted by a dramatic movement to the far right. Only time will tell.

3. *Differences in Recognition of Adulthood.*

It has been said that most young people today have been denied the opportunities of adult responsibility until fairly late in their twenties. This is usually coupled with a reference to the maturing experiences of the Depression of the thirties and the global war of the forties.

This is probably true of a segment of our youth, particularly those who pursue advanced academic degrees. It is not true of the ghetto child, who certainly has simulated for him most of the

Living with Militancy in Our Schools

experiences of an economic depression. Nor is it true of the youth who is sent to Viet Nam to fight our most frustrating war.

There is a great difference, however, in the *privileges* of adulthood as they are extended in colleges as contrasted with secondary schools. As indicated above, the differences between college youth and high school youth seem to prescribe that the latter are treated as large children rather than as young adults.

In his anthology of the contemporary high school underground press, edited soon after his own high school graduation, John Birmingham puts it this way [2]:

> ... They accuse groups such as SDS of organizing small groups of high school students. You can see how wrong this is—how ignorant it is of the gap between the SDS generation and ours— ...

He referred to an interview of a student leader in the high school underground press of a large city, who made it eloquently and bluntly clear that college movements had no influence on their movement.

WHY OUR SECONDARY SCHOOLS?

A high school should be a microcosm, a valid slice of community life. Today's high school is not quite that. Some reasons for this are totally commendable.

The state of community life in America today is not always worthy of imitation in a school. Misguided permissiveness by some and disregard of law by others are clearly and adversely affecting our life style. The secondary school principal cannot simply accept a duplication of everything as it actually is in the community to be encouraged in his school. Sometimes it seems to me that the only person left in American society who says *no* to adolescents is the secondary school principal. Even he is forced into what is hopefully a campaign of orderly retreat. He need not accept complete defeat, however, if he can distinguish carefully between the significant and the trivial. Relinquishing his role as an arbiter of fashion in clothing and hair style may

---

[2] John Birmingham (ed.), *Our Time Is Now. Notes from the High School Underground.* (New York, Praeger Publishers, 1970), p. 42.

permit him to retain a role as an agent of positive change in school *and* community.

Some reasons for the high school's image as an island of repression and reaction in the community are not acceptable. Oppressive rules, smothering bureaucracy, and rigid resistance to change are often tolerated because of administrative convenience in dealing with large numbers of students, many of whom are alienated by the atmosphere which is created to contain them. The more a student reacts against his bonds, the tighter the knots are tied.

Reckless adventures into freedom for students have all but ruined some high schools. Anarchy is no responsible alternative to totalitarianism. Responsible democracy may be, but we have seldom given it a chance. In the meantime, students are demanding to be heard. They feel that they know what is wrong. To date, they have not addressed themselves seriously to reasonable and specific alternatives. We still have a choice.

HOW LONG WILL IT LAST?

History teaches us of the impermanence of strong movements that require sustained effort and dedication. Opinions vary on the future of youth militancy, but those who think it will simply disappear sound to me like wishful thinkers. Confrontation politics has resulted in too many gains for too many groups (of all ages) to expect that it will be abandoned as a means of expediting change. Militancy will probably vary in intensity from time to time and from place to place, but it certainly will not disappear from the American scene until substantial reforms have eliminated injustice for all the segments of our society. This includes students. The only alternative would seem to be strong repressive measures which are hopefully alien to our way of life. Only by addressing ourselves with determination and courage to the frustrations of expediting change, can we make our schools into places of trust and truth and *eliminate the need for excessive militancy*. The weed must be attacked at its roots.

WHAT ARE THE ISSUES?

A great deal has been written about issues in secondary school protests. On larger issues, they seem to follow the general pattern of college protests: racism, poverty in "prosperity," unemployment, war, the industrial-military establishment, the credibility gap (which is a tap root of the generation gap; they simply cannot believe their elders), ecology, etc. An emphasis, however, is more sharply directed at the operational aspects of their own schools: irrelevance of curriculum; uninspired and downright bad teaching; oppressive regulations (especially in reference to clothing and hair style); censorship of student views; no real voice for students in school affairs; and downright pervasive boredom throughout the total school experience.

Secondary students, especially in larger schools, seem to feel that their individuality is swallowed up by the institution itself. They become holes in data cards, not people. Changes and improvements seem to take forever. Incomprehensible excuses are given for not making changes: tenure laws, lack of funds, school board policies, state regulations.

Perhaps the single strongest thread that runs through all these issues can be simply stated—poor communications between administration and staff, administration and students, teachers and students, school and community. Here, at least, is something we can see and understand, something we can handle!

WHAT FORMS HAS MILITANCY ASSUMED?

Let us turn briefly to the format of protest. Following this listing, specific preventive techniques will be suggested for each.

One area in which high school youth has readily and openly imitated college students, in form if not degree, is in the format of protest. The key concept in protest is *confrontation*. This process of bringing together groups with varying goals and interests to exchange ideas can vary from calm discussions to emotional clashes involving harsh words and even physical violence.

The tendency seems to be away from the small, formally elected committees seated face to face. Today a confrontation group may consist of everyone who is angry enough and vocal enough or concerned enough to attend a showdown with another group or with an authority group.

An extreme example of a violent confrontation of two groups (both opposed to actions and/or attitudes of authority figures for different reasons) was reported in the *New York Times* on the day following a massive youth demonstration against the extension of the Viet Nam War into Cambodia and in protest to the killing of four Kent State College students.[3]

WAR FOES HERE ATTACKED BY CONSTRUCTION WORKERS
CITY HALL IS STORMED

> Helmeted construction workers broke up a student anti-war demonstration in Wall Street yesterday, chasing youths through the canyons of the financial district in a wild noontime melee that left about 70 persons injured.

More often confrontations are peaceful and reasonable. Teachers, students, and administrators, for example, may gather to discuss needed changes in a marking system. Techniques of confrontation vary. Our most radical students usually believe that unless power is seized through force, it has no meaning. Power that is given to students without pressure being applied to obtain it has no significance. Liberal administrators feel that changes for the good can be appreciably hastened by the use of peaceful confrontation techniques. One very important fact to remember is that *confrontation tactics have a remarkable record of success in America in the past decade.*

Each form of protest is directed to confronting someone in some way with the opinions of the protesting group. The most common forms that have been attempted in secondary schools are:

The Rumble or Riot

Most often this is a racial phenomenon in which the school is selected for a battleground. There may be no serious complaints

---

[3] *New York Times,* Saturday, May 9, 1970, p. 1. Article by Homer Bigart.

Living with Militancy in Our Schools

by either side against the school. It is simply a convenient place to muster forces for battle. Both sides show up in battle dress, armed according to local customs.

This is easily the most dangerous and the most intolerable form of confrontation our schools have faced. Innocent bystanders have been killed and injured. All of us who work in the schools have an inescapable responsibility for the safety of our students. Drastic and far-reaching steps must be taken to prevent riots in our schools and stop them if they do start. Specific recommendations will be listed later in this chapter.

The Boycott of Classes

A group of students or the entire student body may remain in the building but refuse to go to classes. Usually they gather in the halls, the auditorium, the cafeteria, etc. Quite often this form of protest is a spur-of-the-moment phenomenon, directed at a specific recent situation, sometimes relatively minor in nature, such as an unfortunate public statement by a teacher or an administrator.

The Strike and Picketing

A student strike usually involves rather widespread planning for at least a few days in advance. It may be directed against the school, but more often it is part of a broader effort, for example a protest against war or environmental pollution. School authorities usually know that it is coming.

The Seizure of Spaces

College students have set a precedent of seizing and occupying buildings and offices, usually administrative quarters, to force a showdown confrontation. Quite often vandalism and rifling of files is part of the routine. This is relatively rare in high schools since administrative areas are usually too small to hold many students.

The Slowdown

This is primarily an annoyance technique, most often employed by a given group (such as a racial minority) protesting what they consider to be unfair practices. The procedure is simple. Students get to classes late all day long.

The Underground Press

Usually badly written and ineptly produced underground newspapers have become a growing secondary school phenomenon in recent years. Drearily imitative of college efforts, most of them turn to garbled facts and shocking language to attract readers. Since sustained effort, talent, and funds are needed to keep them alive, many of them expire rapidly.

The best ones seem to appear in urban schools and in the schools of our most affluent suburbs, and some of these are excellent in many ways. The John Birmingham book cited earlier in the chapter contains examples of very fine writing and very mature thinking by young men and women in our secondary schools. If nothing else, they are evidence of some effective teaching of English in these school districts.

Vandalism and Sabotage

A small percentage of our shockingly accelerated amount of vandalism of school property results from sheer childish mischief. Another segment can be attributed to twisted minds. Much of it, however, must be interpreted as a form of protest. The vandal is usually trying to say something.

Recently the most radical elements of the youth rebellion have turned to extremism in sabotage to strike at the Establishment. Burning and bombing (often ineptly) seem to be "the thing" of the lunatic fringe. *We cannot assume that they will not strike at an occupied school building.* Fanaticism seems to have no limits.

HOW CAN WE CONTAIN MILITANCY AND CHANNEL IT INTO POSITIVE DIRECTIONS?

One of the most difficult lessons for educators to learn is that *it can happen here!* The most disheartening phenomenon in this age of revolt is the nearly universal refusal of educators to accept the idea that student disorder can happen in *their* school until it has actually happened. The record is dismal in school district after school district, in community after community; no preparation, no preventive measures, no valid attempts to make

Living with Militancy in Our Schools

necessary changes unless and until the lid has blown off. This is precisely why young people and some not-so-young groups have turned to militant confrontation as a way of life, *simply because it works* when normal channels of protest have failed.

Once we recognize the fact that it *can* happen to us, we must direct ourselves to the root causes, taking an objective look at our entire establishment, guided by the experiences of other districts which have lived through one or more types of revolt. American schools are more remarkable for their sameness than for their differences. This is particularly true of their weaknesses. Finding our faults should be no great mystery. We are usually painfully aware of them and woefully slow about eliminating them.

Then we move on to a careful study of the symptoms of unrest: increases in violations of discipline; high absenteeism; increasing numbers of dropouts; higher frustration among teachers of slower-learning classes; more quarreling and fighting among students; an increase in sullen attitudes and unwillingness to communicate on the part of students; etc. These symptoms often build up so slowly that we are unaware of them until it is too late. We must share our reactions with our colleagues in an effort to improve our sensitivities. This is the school's radar equipment to prevent collision.

Most important of all, we must *improve communications in every direction.* It is usually not adequate to utilize existing channels and organizations. New ones must be created. Let's be specific and honest. The American high school Student Council has, at the time of this writing, an extremely bad image in the minds of many students. Most of the fault for this can be placed squarely on teachers and administrators. Given very little authority to deal with any but the most trivial matters, guided and directed by heavy faculty hands, Student Councils create an image of a company union, a tool of the Establishment.

Council members are frequently selected, directly or indirectly, by teachers and administrators. Criteria for membership often include arbitrary academic achievement levels. Thus Student Council members tend to be students who have had the greatest success with the system (however bad it may be), who are the most articulate, and who have the least complaints about their school. Turning to them for a true assessment of student opinion is about as effective as asking the Chamber of Commerce to summarize what people are really thinking about in a local ghetto.

Student Councils must be reformed and they can be, but in the meantime, the wise administrator will turn to supplementary channels of communication with students. This can be as simple a matter as having lunch with a randomly selected group of students. It can be more carefully planned, but *to place total reliance on the simple process of election by peer groups is not enough.* "What peer groups? Grade levels? Classes?" More and more, schools are examining this question with care. One of the more promising developments has come from the idea that student representatives should have maximal *out-of-school* contact with those whom they represent. This means elections by community geography, neighborhoods, "turfs."

A very common mistake made by administrators is to assume that ethnic and racial groups comprise single unified communities. More frequently, there are *several* black communities, for example, in a given school district. This should be studied carefully by faculty members who know the entire community best, but students should have a decisive role in the format of representative councils.

The same may be true of adult groups. In some cases PTA's have problems quite similar to those outlined above for Student Councils. *Good communications begin with the assumption that you are communicating with the right people.*

Preventing riots is the single most important task of the school staff. This can usually be done when the danger signals are detected early enough. Leaders of the groups involved are almost always easy to identify. They are usually proud of their status and loath to deny it.

Bring together the leaders of the opposing factions with one or two level-headed faculty members (preferably teachers whom they trust and/or admire) and begin an open-ended discussion that explores every avenue of solution. This conference should not conclude without a guarantee that the safety of students in the school will not be endangered by any physical confrontation in the school. Failing this, all leaders should be suspended from school until they are ready to make such commitments.

One clothing regulation that must be rigidly enforced is the refusal to permit into the school any student in battle dress. Teachers and administrators who have experience with youth gangs can quickly recognize the uniform: a sweat shirt with sleeves removed, a wide belt with a large buckle, tight dungarees, and sneakers.

The use of uniformed police should be studied with great care, but when the situation becomes dangerous they should be called. At this point the principal must turn over command to the ranking police officer involved.

School personnel must understand that many police officials resent the attitudes of school administrators, and often school officials are fearful of police overreaction in crises involving students. This varies greatly from place to place, but overreaction of police seems greatest in areas where their salaries and general support are lowest. Communities get what they pay for. Major efforts must be made at all levels, particularly at the top, for a complete understanding between school people and police. This is best accomplished on a one-to-one basis (police chief and principal or superintendent), preferably in an informal setting such as over lunch or coffee.

In every school district, there are teachers who cannot deal successfully with crises and other teachers who are extremely effective even in the middle of a full-blown riot. The latter can be more effective in some situations than uniformed police since they work with these students every day. They know most of them. They can identify them.

When a school district recognizes the faintest possibility of a riot, a careful plan should be prepared to relieve a group of the most effective riot-control teachers for immediate transfer to the scene of trouble. Very often this will be a cafeteria, especially in a large school. The size of this group will depend upon the size of the student body in the troubled school. Teachers may be selected from any level, any specialty, any building. The only criteria should be effectiveness in crisis and a willingness to serve. Simple exchanges can be made in an emergency.

Supervisors without teaching duties can be used in emergency situations or to relieve other teachers for those stations. The important thing is that when the emergency condition and station is announced, everyone will know precisely what to do and where to go. A single telephone call by a beleaguered principal should result in immediate relief. Often the plan, if executed *before* the trouble starts, can prevent it from happening. Significantly, extended coverage of corridors and other non-teaching spaces by teachers *who know what they are doing* will almost always prevent a riot, unless the vast majority of the entire school is involved. In that case, the police must be called and school must be closed until the underlying problems are solved. If an entire student body is prepared to take physical action against a school, something very, very serious is wrong with that school.

Boycotts of classes can usually be "talked out" if the administration and teachers are *really* willing to listen. Students are almost always reasonable if their sense of justice is not outraged. An appeal for time to investigate the cause and a promise to report the findings in full to all students in one or more assemblies is usually the correct approach. Attempts to withhold facts, however, can be extremely dangerous.

Student strikes, like all strikes, present more complicated problems. If the issues are school generated, the same procedure outlined above for boycotts may be followed. If they are issues over which the school has no control, more positive alternatives can be suggested to the students.

The administrator can make it clear, for example, that a strike has at least two disadvantages for those who advocate it. First, all students will probably not support it. Many will simply stay home. Others will become bored and seek other diversions. Secondly, school will have to be in session extra days into the normal vacation period or periods to make up for the lost time.

Involvement days have become increasingly popular. On these days teachers and students will meet in classrooms as usual, but by mutual consent they may suspend the regular lesson in order to discuss the matter of concern to students. Speakers or films could be used to supply added information. Given a high degree of student motivation, a great deal of learning often

Living with Militancy in Our Schools

results. The result can also be a massive waste of time. It all depends upon organization and administrative control.

Seizure of spaces cannot be tolerated. Reason with patience should be given every chance for success. Promises of open-ended discussion of issues can be made. Failing this, the law should be enforced, hopefully with restraint and common sense.

Slowdowns can be handled in the same manner as boycotts. They are usually caused by similar grievances.

The underground press evokes a variety of responses among school administrators who have experienced them. Some of the extremes may be easily summarized:

1. Ignore them (but read them to see what they say about you). They require sustained effort and funds. Students seldom have either.
2. Wipe them out. Expel the editors and publishers.

Perhaps the gravest danger here is overreaction on the part of administrators. Providing that the same restraints involving falsehood, bad taste, and defamation of character that apply to all commercial newspapers are invoked, what is really wrong with a little competition for the officially sanctioned school publication? After all, an underground newspaper is usually started because the official school paper is heavily censored and/or deadly dull. The best way to prevent these publications is to adopt a reasonable attitude toward them and give reasonable support to the regular publication.

When the underground press surfaces, a just and reasonable attitude toward it on the part of the administration will disappoint any of its staff striving merely to gain attention through shock. It will also prepare the entire student body to be reasonable when and if an issue must be suppressed because of violation of legal or other restraints, with which all newspapers must learn to live.

PLANNING AHEAD FOR TROUBLE

All school districts should have policies and regulations stating school board positions on all possible manifestations of student militancy. These will be treated in a later chapter, along with sample policies and regulations. Also needed, however, is a manual of emergency procedures for every employee of the district.

The following is a suggested outline of procedures which may be helpful in preparing such an emergency checklist. Much of the material has been derived from such a checklist developed by Dr. Irving Karam, Schools Superintendent of the Council Rock District in Bucks County, Pennsylvania. Since this document was prepared for a specific situation in a specific district, it has been broadened and added to for broader application.

1. *Introduction.* Make it clear precisely what the document is and how it is to be used. Remember that as soon as it is distributed it will fall into student hands and be analyzed carefully by activist leaders for statements that can be used to convince students of administrative repression. Examine every sentence *out of context*. Stress the ultimate goal of *safety of students*. Do not editorialize in this document.

2. *Police Liaison.* This is no place to discuss agreements and arrangements with the police. Simply list telephone numbers and procedures and conditions under which *direct* calls (as opposed to going through a communications center) may be made. Also list numbers and procedures for calling fire departments, ambulance services, and other emergency services.

3. *Personnel Orientation.* Orientation sessions in relatively small groups (under 100) should be held by administrators *after* they have had a chance to read the checklist. All questions must be answered clearly. If the document contains a segment that is confusing, the entire document should be rewritten and reissued, with a revision date prominently displayed. A revision containing significant changes should be printed on paper of a different color than the original. All outdated manuals should be destroyed after a revision has been distributed.

An effort to conduct "business as usual" should be stressed. Schools should only be closed on direct orders from the superintendent or his designated deputy.

Pertinent laws and policies should be briefly summarized. Employees should be discouraged from use of force, except when it is necessary to prevent injury. Arrests should be made by the police.

A group of teachers with photography skills should be equipped with cameras and films and assigned to take pictures of students, especially when they are agitating or breaking the law. This can be a powerful deterrent to foolish behavior.

All persons with special assignments need to be briefed verbally and fully.

Industrial arts teachers and others who work with dangerous and/or expensive equipment should be prepared to secure this equipment. Arrangements should be made to guard it.

Emergency chain of command must be spelled out. If uniformed police are involved, the resultant command situation must be explained to school personnel.

Transportation personnel must be alerted for emergency dismissal.

4. *Communications.* Each school must have a communications center and the district must have one. Several "rumor clinic" numbers should be established to keep the basic lines clear. Calls for information should be directed to rumor clinic numbers, and persons manning those stations must be kept informed. If separate lines are available close to the command centers, these would be the best rumor clinic stations.

Walkie-talkies and bullhorns in good working condition should be available.

Pay stations in schools should be guarded or deactivated to prevent calls for outside reinforcements or calls from hysterical persons with incomplete information or misinformation to fearful parents or friends. The telephone company should be consulted on how to do this.

5. *Building Security.* A primary concern must be to keep unauthorized people out of the building. If the district requires visitors' passes, this is easy. Secondary schools have many doors. Each door must be covered during emergencies. Teachers who work in the building can do this job best, but if custodians or nonprofessionals can be used it will relieve teachers for more critical duties.

Certain doors can be designated for authorized entrances or exits.

6. *Public Information.* Two or more administrators in positions to know the facts should release information to press and radio. They should be certain to indicate *before and within* the message, the time and date it is being released. Often radio stations record statements over and over throughout the day. When events happen swiftly, an earlier statement is interpreted by many as a deliberate lie because it is not up to date. People should be asked *not* to call the school during the emergency. Alternative (rumor clinic) numbers should be given out.

Preaddressed and stamped envelopes for all parents should be ready for a rapid summary that should be prepared as soon as the emergency ends.

7. *Miscellaneous.* Maintain communications with student leaders as closely as possible.

Make no concessions in the midst of confrontation. Request written "demands" for later discussion.

Maintain contact with neighboring districts.

Keep a log of events with times indicated and, if possible, identification of persons involved as well as witnesses.

Identify agitators and radicals and attempt to get them into the school office for lengthy questioning without martyrizing them. Have them arrested if they are seen breaking any law.

Establish first aid stations in key positions.

Have sandwiches and coffee taken to employees who cannot leave duty posts.

If you intend to liberalize any procedure or practice which you feel is unfair, *do it now before a confrontation is necessary!*

The tone of this document is authoritarian. It must be. It is to be used in emergencies which do not lend themselves to committee deliberations. *Democracy returns when discussions are held after the emergency is over.*

3

> There is no drug problem at the universities abroad . . . That is an American problem . . .
>
> Joseph A. Califano, Jr.[1]

Coping with the Narcotics Problem

It is important to remember the rapid changes which are taking place in the youth movement and especially in the drug scene. The above quotation is significant in that it was a precise statement of fact at the time it was published. Only a few months later Britain, Canada, and other nations began to experience a growing drug problem, especially among their young. Whether or not this continues, it remains at the time of this writing a serious problem in America.

---

[1] Califano, J. A., *The Student Revolution, A Global Confrontation* (New York, W. W. Norton and Company, Inc., 1970), p. 60.

ANOTHER AMERICAN DILEMMA

A most disturbing crisis of the sixties, which has continued into the seventies, was the wildly accelerating abuse among young people of all types of street drugs, of pills and combinations of pills, and most especially of marijuana. By the close of the decade, the problem had become an avalanche that blanketed most of America. Beginning in our large-city ghettos and among our urban poor, drug abuse spread rapidly out through the suburbs into our rural regions. It spread upward from the lowest social class to the highest. Most frightening of all, it spread downward through our age groups deep into our elementary schools.

By 1970 recorded deaths from heroin use alone in New York City reached 224 (for the previous year).[2] Of this number, 55 were children under 17 and *one was 12 years old*. Many trends had become apparent in our schools. Some of these were: (1) an estimated 20% to 60% of suburban high school students had tried marijuana at least once; (2) the use of some type of drug had become a strong "in thing" in secondary schools; (3) the use of hard narcotics in secondary schools varied according to availability (usually meaning proximity to larger cities) rather than to choice, while college students were turning away from hard drugs and moving heavily into the use of marijuana; (4) the problem of finding and convicting pushers had become extremely difficult; (5) parents were beginning to become alarmed but generally refused to accept the idea that *their* children could be involved; (6) young people were becoming very skeptical of traditional narcotics education and rejected significantly the warnings posted against marijuana.

Educators were beginning to see that drug abuse was a *group* problem as well as a problem for the individual. They realized the importance of finding answers for the question, "Why are they doing this?" Perhaps the closest parallel in American history can be found in the decade of the twenties, when the drinking of bootleg alcohol was the vogue among American students down to and including the secondary schools.

---

[2] Richard D. Lyons, "Heroin: Teen-agers to the Morgue," *New York Times*, February 1, 1970, Medicine column.

The application of lessons from the twenties and thirties to our problem of the seventies must be handled with care. The widespread drinking fad among students declined sharply after Prohibition was repealed in 1932, but we must bear in mind the effects of the severe and prolonged economic Depression that set in at about the same time. A serious lack of money by students in that earlier period may well have helped to curb alcohol abuse and even cigarette smoking. It would probably be an error to assume that legalization of marijuana would reduce the problem. Legalization would, as was the case in 1932, improve the *quality* of the available product and reduce the dangers of amateur chemistry, but today's affluent kids, faced with a plentiful supply of legal and high-grade marijuana, would almost certainly not reduce their consumption of the popular weed.

A more appropriate lesson from bootleg days might be taken from the crude nature of alcohol education in that period. Drinking was labelled as a *moral* problem as well as a medical one. Drinking was considered to be a disease in itself rather than a possible symptom of an emotional problem. The puritanical pitch to the young was largely centered around the conviction that almost anything pleasant except eating was sinful. As the elderly salvationist says in *Guys and Dolls,* "Coffee is *so* good. It's a wonder it isn't a sin!" Intelligent youngsters in the early thirties did not create a revolution but they developed a significant cynicism toward the preaching of their elders on almost any subject. This was due to the fact that they had been lied to so often.

The current generation gap is also largely a credibility gap. Today's kids have also been lied to on many important matters, especially marijuana. The key to good communications between elders and youth is really so simple—tell the truth! Lies have failed as they always do when told to human beings who are naive enough or brave enough to cling to high ideals.

THE MARIJUANA CONTROVERSY

The marijuana which is smoked American style is traditionally cut from the flowering and leaves of the hemp plant. The plant has been hung upside down for a drying period during which the juices seep down into the usable portion. The plant itself can grow like a weed almost anywhere. Before sisal and synthetic substitutes came into use, hemp was widely grown throughout the world as fiber for rope and cloth. The by-product in various forms was sold legitimately as a therapeutic drug. In 1937, an American tax law made it unprofitable for the pharmaceutical industry to continue converting marijuana into a commercial drug.

The fact that marijuana, commonly called "pot," can be very easily grown and converted into a smokable product makes it most difficult to control. Heroin famines can be created temporarily by seizures of large shipments, but this is impossible to do with a product that can be grown in almost any backyard garden.

The widespread use of marijuana within the middle class of America, and not merely among its younger members, became an established fact in the late sixties. In one week in February, 1970, marijuana arrests included some sons of very prominent Americans. It is ironic to note that when marijuana moved up into the middle and higher classes, one of its nicknames changed from weed to grass.

If we want to tell the truth about marijuana to our students, what shall we say? Let us begin with some facts we must first understand, facts which are generally accepted by science today. Unpleasant as their acceptance may be to elders, they are known to be facts by the young:

1. Under *most conditions* for *most people,* marijuana does not *seem* to be dangerous. It is not *physically* habit forming and does not necessarily lead to the use of more dangerous drugs.
2. On the hard evidence currently available, marijuana is less harmful than alcohol or tobacco.
3. Without any scientific basis, the American public has been led to believe that marijuana is a dangerous, addictive drug which stimulates crimes of violence and increases sexual drive to a point beyond ordinary control.
4. The only truly comprehensive study of the relationship of marijuana to crime was initiated in 1938 by Mayor La Guardia of New York. A committee of scientists reported,

among other things, that: (a) in most instances, the behavior of the marijuana smoker was of a friendly, sociable nature; (b) there was no direct relationship between the commission of crimes of violence and the use of marijuana; (c) smoking marijuana can be stopped abruptly with no resulting mental or physical distress; (d) marijuana itself has no specific stimulant effect in regard to sexual desires or ability; (e) no evidence was found of an acquired tolerance for marijuana; (f) no mental or physical deterioration could be attributed to the drug; (g) the lessening of inhibitions and repression, the euphoric state, the feeling of adequacy, the freer expression of thoughts and ideas, and the increase of appetite for food brought about by marijuana, suggested therapeutic possibilities.

I do not propose that these facts be repeated in drug education, but that they be borne in mind by the educator who is to be involved in the preparation and/or presentation of such education. Students already know them. The real problem lies in immature interpretations of these facts and the refusal to believe other facts which should discourage the use of marijuana, especially by the young.

What, then, can we say without widening the credibility gap? Here are some examples of central themes that can be safely used in educating students about marijuana:

• *The scientific evidence on marijuana is not all in yet.* The active chemical ingredient in marijuana, tetrahydrocannabinol, has only been available for study since 1966. Conclusive evidence has not yet been published, but many preliminary opinions on possible dangers connected with the use of marijuana have been voiced by scientists. Marijuana literature can be prepared on two bases: *What we know* and *what we have reason to suspect*. If properly labelled, both categories should receive various consideration by most students.

What Do We Know?

• *We know that the possession of marijuana, even in minute quantities, is against the federal law.* Although penalties were reduced in 1970, the new law still provides a penalty of not more than one year imprisonment and/or a fine of $1000 for a first or second offense. The third offense increases the risk to a maximum of not more than three years imprisonment and/or a $10,000 fine.

Selling or *giving* drugs to anyone under 21 by anyone over 18 is treated far more seriously than possession. A first offense may lead to imprisonment for not more than ten years and/or a fine of not more than $20,000.

It may be a good idea, where such things are permitted, to arrange tours of a prison by students at the high school level. This can be a sobering if not frightening experience. The important point to stress, however, in connection with drug abuse or the breaking of laws in any form of demonstration or protest, is *the tremendous handicap of carrying a record of a conviction for a felony* throughout life. Poor judgment or rash behavior at an early age can eliminate many future opportunities in life. A recorded conviction can prevent a person from entering most organized professions, such as education, medicine, law, or accounting. It can prevent public office holding. It would almost certainly cut off responsible positions in private sectors of employment. Governmental employment would be out because it is always preceded by background research. Certain types of licenses (such as liquor licenses) necessary for the operation of businesses may be denied. Police work, private or public, would be out of the question. Each school district in preparing literature on drugs should research local ordinances and state law for information of this type. They can provide very compelling arguments against the current trend to break "unjust" laws.

• *We know that cheap substances of all types are used by suppliers to dilute drugs for more profit.* It is not uncommon for young people to purchase what they think is marijuana and receive only herbs or weeds. Who knows what inhaling the smoke of unknown weeds and herbs can do to the lungs?

• *We know that buyers of illegal marijuana have no knowledge of the strength of the substance they have purchased, and that heavy dosage can be dangerous.* Besides the unknown factor of dilution, there is also an important question of the origins of the marijuana itself. If it comes from Asia, Africa, or the Middle East it will be much stronger than the American product. Even Mexican marijuana can vary tremendously in strength, depending upon where it has been grown and how it has been cut.

• *We know that heavy dosages of marijuana have produced severe reactions in subjects tested.* These reactions included serious emotional upsets such as deep depression and panic.

• *We know that some individuals who have had only mild dosages of marijuana have experienced these same reactions of depression and fear.*

• *We know that continued use of marijuana induces a psychological dependency* which can be as compelling as physical addiction, and which can be harmful to a wholesome personality.

• *We know that regular use of marijuana makes it more difficult to form reasonable decisions, maintain a normal study or work schedule, and pursue truly worthwhile goals.* While the user drops out of the mainstream of life, his peers move ahead.

• *We know that adolescence has enough problems without adding marijuana to the list.* Whatever the scientists eventually discover about the effects of marijuana on the mature body, it is highly doubtful that medical approval will ever be extended for its indiscriminate use by people who are physically or psychologically immature.

• *We know that the constant contact between user and pusher eventually leads to the availability of stronger drugs, and often strong sales pitches for their use by the pusher.* Young and inexperienced people with money are easy prey for salesmen of practically anything.

What Do Scientists Suspect?

Current research in marijuana is taking many directions. Each direction is determined by suspicions or inferences based on existing clues. One can readily assume from the nature of the research and from preliminary conclusions that certain strong possibilities exist:

• That marijuana may lead to birth defects when used by a pregnant woman. This has been established in mice but may or may not be true in humans.

- That severe psychotic reactions have resulted in a few American soldiers in Viet Nam as a result of using marijuana. Vietnamese marijuana is twice as strong as the generally purchased American street variety.
- That it takes more than eight days for the human body to rid itself of all chemical traces of marijuana. This accounts for the "reverse tolerance" experienced by frequent smokers. (Findings released by the National Institute of Mental Health in December, 1970 as reported in a lead editorial in the *Boston Herald Traveler* on Saturday, December 26, 1970.)
- That marijuana *may* have a permanent or long-term bad effect on the body and/or the mind.
- That very likely marijuana has no beneficial effects on creative thinking or creative achievement. Painters and writers who have worked with and without marijuana have not (in the opinions of objective critics) created better products with the aid of marijuana. The danger here lies in the fact that marijuana induces a false sense of adequacy that makes the creative artist and the performer *think they are doing a better job*. It is reasonable to surmise that marijuana may also give the driver a false sense of security behind the wheel. Bad poetry cannot kill, but bad driving can and does.
- That marijuana accumulates in the liver and may cause damage there.
- That large doses may cause serious hallucinations and permanent psychological harm.

Thus we can see that there is no reason to lie about marijuana. *The truth is bad enough*. Our program of education can be built around damaging facts and equally damaging and properly labelled assumptions by scientists, who are working to establish conclusive facts about marijuana.

OTHER DRUGS IN COMMON USE

Marijuana is the greatest headache for educators because it is so readily available to youngsters. Other drugs and stimulants, however, can be far more dangerous when they are available. One can also argue that many prescription pills (uppers

Coping with the Narcotics Problem

and downers) commonly used by adults and many non-prescription pills used in high dosage and in creative combinations, constitute a serious problem today. Some commonly available substances can be purchased almost anywhere and can be far more harmful than marijuana (gasoline and glue sniffing).

Since the schools cannot become medical or therapeutic agencies without weakening their educational functions, we should direct our major attention to classifying drugs and stimulants in terms of symptoms in order to help teachers and administrators identify users so that they may be referred to sources of effective help. Discipline procedures in schools are complicated when teachers know little or nothing about drugs or their symptoms. Far more serious complications may appear when teachers refuse to believe that the drug problem even exists in *their* schools. Often routine disciplinary procedure is used with a student who is under the influence of a dangerous drug. One of the symptoms caused by some drugs is a complete disregard for consequences of actions. Teachers need constant briefing in these matters.

Let us consider the major street drugs in use today, with an emphasis on the symptoms involved.

Narcotic Drugs

This classification involves dangerous and addictive drugs, generally products of opium or chemical by-products originating in the juices of the poppy plant. Some synthetic drugs (such as Demerol) and some drugs derived from opium (such as cocaine) would also fit into this category. Marijuana, although not medically classified as a narcotic drug, is so classified for legal purposes.

Addiction to narcotic drugs is considered a serious illness with a relatively poor prognosis for complete recovery. The process is a familiar one today: temporary escape from tension and anxiety, increasing dependency, increasing required dosage, neglect of other body needs, obsession with obtaining a "fix," greatly increased financial needs to maintain supply, attempted cure with great physical distress, return to normalcy, return to usage, and back through the cycle.

Symptoms of the use of hard narcotics are relatively difficult to hide once the teacher has learned them and accepts the possibility that the problem may exist in his classroom.

Narcotic Drug Symptoms

- Long-sleeved shirts or sweaters worn constantly to hide needle marks.
- Frequent association with known users.
- Constant borrowing of money.
- Petty thievery.
- Appearance alone in secluded places.
- Disappearance from school for short periods.
- Drowsiness and lack of response in the classroom.
- Constant wearing of dark glasses to hide dilated pupils.
- Sharp downward trend in quality and quantity of schoolwork.
- Sharp downgrading of general appearance.

The most common street drug of the narcotic group is heroin. Heroin is illegal for *any* use and while the supply varies according to location and the current status of import flow, it is generally available within a two-hour driving radius of our largest cities. It is used increasingly by secondary school students who can afford its high price. College students, evidently impressed by medical evidence, seem to be avoiding it increasingly along with LSD in favor of marijuana and other milder stimulants.

Hallucinogens

Although the use of the synthetic drug known as LSD in high schools is relatively rare, teachers may encounter a student in a late phase of a "trip" or one who has unwittingly swallowed some of the drug as a result of a prank. Young people have been known to give LSD to friends in candy, cookies, or other edibles. This is usually done at parties, but it may happen during a school session.

The favorite drug of the hippy movement of the fifties (along with marijuana), LSD was finally made illegal after a

Coping with the Narcotics Problem

decade of use. Ironically, its illegality was established at approximately the same time that it had fallen out of favor and out of use with most college students. The medical evidence was in and the college set evidently believed it.

LSD, if used several times, will cause varying degrees of irreversible brain damage, depending upon the dosage and other factors. It imbalances chemicals in the brain tissue and attaches itself to protein in the central nervous system. There are also strong suspicions that birth defects can be caused in babies born to mothers who used LSD.

All the media have exposed the dangers of the bad trip and the superman delusions which could inspire the user to attempt to fly through an open window at any height. Police records in large cities include case after case of incredibly reckless driving caused by drug abuse.

It seems obvious that if LSD can be injurious to a mature brain, it must be even more harmful to a growing brain. Drug education has no need to turn to half-truths about LSD. The truth is frightening enough to impress college students. The emphasis must be placed now at the lower levels.

Hallucinogen Symptoms

- A trance-like appearance.
- Manifestations of sudden fear or terror.
- Rapid emotional changes.
- Little or no interest in the activity of the group.
- Failure to respond to questions or participate in conversation.

Stimulant Drugs (Uppers)

Stimulants are very commonly used by adults to fend off weariness (as on long drives) and to assist in weight reduction. Common stimulants are amphetamine, dextroamphetamine, and methamphetamine, commonly called "bennies" or "speed." Moderately prescribed dosage produces sensations of good health and normal well-being in an otherwise weary body. Heavier dosage causes extreme tension with very bad aftereffects. Taken as a street drug, dosage is almost always heavy with dangerous aftereffects. Heart action and metabolic processes (conversion of food into chemical energy) is greatly increased. Serious psychological difficulties result from continued overdosage.

Stimulant Overdosage Symptoms

- Tension and extreme irritability.
- Garbled speech and incoherency.
- Disorganized thinking.
- Too much physical activity.
- Dilated pupils.
- Inability to eat and sleep.
- Continuous urge to chain smoke.

Depressant Drugs (Downers)

Depressants or sedatives are manufactured to relax the central nervous system. The most commonly used are barbiturates such as Nembutal, Seconal, and phenobarbital. The favorite street term for them is "goofballs."

Used medically in moderation for high blood pressure, epilepsy, and other diseases which are controlled by inducing relaxation, they slow the heart rate and breathing. Taken in overdosage, as they usually are in street use, they induce similar symptoms to the overuse of alcohol. Like alcohol, they can easily become addictive and dangerous and lead to anti-social behavior.

Depressant Overdosage Symptoms

- Similar to alcohol intoxication without alcohol breath.
- Lack of interest in normal activities.
- "Goofy" behavior and speech.
- Falling asleep at unlikely times and in unlikely places.

AN ACTION PROGRAM FOR SCHOOLS

Schools cannot solve the drug problem alone, but they have some rather clear responsibilities. First there is the responsibility to uphold the law, to prevent the sale and use of drugs in and around the schools. Secondly, schools are responsible for an effective program of education that will give students the knowledge and desire to avoid drug usage. To date the

Coping with the Narcotics Problem

record of our schools in carrying out these responsibilities is not good.

Formidable problems lie behind this failure. When we seek answers to the most important question, "Why?", we are faced with an open Pandora's box of societal problems over which we school people have little or no control. Young people who use drugs are often alienated from society for reasons that are understandable. We may not see the need for the alienation but we must realize the legitimacy of their criticism. They see no hope and so they drop out or do battle against the Establishment. We see little hope for massive reform, so we shrug or we "light one little candle rather than curse the darkness." But there is one area in which we can act. We must find the courage to correct with greater haste the weaknesses and inequities in our public schools. We know they exist, we know basically what they are, and we know what is needed to correct them. But we are slow to act. Schools are slow to change. In later chapters, specific recommendations will be made for these needed changes.

The problems of policing, protecting students from pushers, stopping the flow of drugs have been compounded by new laws and new interpretations of old laws. An example would be the current views held by courts on search and seizure. No longer may a principal or teacher search students or their desks and lockers with impunity. Proper procedures must be followed. These procedures need not be intolerable, however. Here we can learn a lesson from police procedures. Simply ask any police officer about this procedure if you have not had an opportunity to observe it. When an officer questions a suspect, he will generally have him empty his pockets onto a table or desk in the presence of principal witnesses. The first offender may protest, but the seasoned criminal does this quickly and automatically without a murmur. If the principal would follow this procedure, there should be no problem in searching a locker when there is reason to believe that something is wrong. If anything remotely resembling narcotics is discovered, the police should be called immediately.

The police have, understandably, a central concern for arresting pushers. Sometimes this effort collides with attempts of school people to assist the addicts. Students who know users generally want to find help for them, but they are very reluctant to name them if there is a chance that this will result in arrest.

Every school district should have a carefully planned and continuous program of drug education that will involve parents, teachers, the police, and, of course, students, in both the teaching and the learning.

RECOMMENDED PROGRAM ELEMENTS

One professional person, with reasonable time available, should be in full charge of the drug education program. He should, if possible, also head up the education program in alcohol and tobacco. Ideally he should be a physical education or health educator, but this is not absolutely necessary. If a district is large enough or the problem is large enough, a full-time job is indicated.

This person should direct the gathering of the best current information and have the authority and support (financial and otherwise) to seek the most effective channels of communication in the community and the school.

- He should have direct and constant contact with all agencies concerned with the problem, including "halfway houses" that assist addicts in finding their way back to a normal life; private and governmental agencies attempting to cure addicts; and any and all means of assistance available.
- He should form separate and continuing committees of community volunteer helpers, parents, teachers, and students concerned with the problem.
- He should promote a continuing program of presentation of facts and advice in the schools and the community.
- He should maintain close and constant liaison with the police, state and local.
- He should work with school administrators in mutual support to attack the problem in both preventive and remedial approaches.
- He should fight for reforms of conditions which lead to alienation of youth and drug abuse.

- He should recommend action programs, such as outdoor education, recreation, and other activities, which offer positive alternatives to the drug culture.

Let me stress the warning implied above that *the campaign against drugs should not be strengthened at the expense of a meaningful program of alcohol and tobacco education.* There seems to be a dangerous tendency to minimize the latter programs due to the greater fear induced by the growing popularity of drugs. Parents of high school youngsters seem to have become fatalists about the use of cigarettes and alcohol by young people. The medical evidence on cigarettes is firmly established today. We have a continuing responsibility to prevent addiction by our students.

Alcohol continues to be a problem in the secondary schools. Among the poor in medium-sized cities which are removed from major urban centers of drug supply, cheap wine and beer and combinations of various types are the most popular stimulants used by youngsters. Here, again, overdosage leads to great problems, especially if intoxicated youngsters drive.

Dr. David C. Lewis, Assistant Professor of Medicine at Harvard Medical School [3], suggests the following guidelines to organizing a drug curriculum:

1. Assess the level of your students' sophistication about drugs.
2. Involve students in planning.
3. Include alcohol and tobacco in your discussion of drug abuse.
4. Compare drug use and abuse.
5. Do not sensationalize.
6. Make drug education part of an ongoing classroom experience.
7. Include experimental data in the drug curriculum.
8. Emphasize the motivational factors that affect a student's decision to use drugs.

---

[3] David C. Lewis, "Preventing Drug Abuse in Schools," The Bulletin of the National Association of Secondary School Principals, Vol. 54, No. 346, May, 1970, pp. 43–52.

9. Don't forget to discuss factors that inhibit the use of drugs.

10. Include the comments of drug-experienced young people in the educational process.

THE ROLE OF THE TEACHER

There are no words which can overemphasize the importance of the classroom teacher in the war against drug abuse. The teacher's attitude toward the problem can cause great positive or negative influence in molding the attitudes of students, particularly the younger ones. Thus it is acutely critical that the administration provide an enlightened drug education for teachers. Teachers must know the facts. There is not the slightest excuse for an American teacher today not to be informed *accurately* about street drugs.

The older teacher is in a position to widen the credibility gap if he persists in repeating untruths and half-truths about drugs. The young teacher is in a position to create enormous harm if he communicates cynicism about drug education or minimizes the harmful effects of drug abuse. This is particularly true if the young teacher makes reference to widespread use of drugs on the college campus he has recently left. He is now a teacher, not a student. Whether he wants to change the Establishment or not, *he is now a member of it*. In any case, a teacher needs only *to communicate the truth,* as it has been established by qualified scientists, not by a subculture of the young.

There is no easy road to victory in the frustrating battle against drug abuse. Persistence in telling the truth may be the key weapon here.

4

> Do unto others as you would have them do unto you.
>
> **Jesus Christ**

The Teacher Works with Militant Youth

The ultimate payoff of our entire educational establishment is the interaction between student and teacher in the classroom. This chapter concerns itself with the role of the teacher in the classroom today, the attitudes and skills he brings with him, and the broad purposes which shape his decision making as he faces increasingly troubled and angry students.

American public schools have been increasingly on the defensive since the time of *Sputnik I*. As we moved into the seventies, a new keynote word crept into our jargon—*accountability*. Our nearly automatic practice of blaming the home and other institutions of society for our own failures is beginning to create a credibility gap that can only harm our schools. A new demand for specific and honest accountability is replacing the vague dissatisfactions of the past. This mounting criticism of our schools is not merely coming from the usual critics and frustrated taxpayers. It is coming from two new sources: from our courts, and from our consumers themselves—our students.

IT ALL STARTS IN THE CLASSROOM

There is little real value in sorting out varying degrees of blame for our shortcomings and assigning these to teachers, administrators, school boards, taxpayers, parents, and students. We must, rather, start with an honest acceptance of the facts. Our worst public schools are unspeakably bad. Most are dreary monuments to mediocrity. We have failed signally to make changes *in areas we control* broadly enough or swiftly enough to meet the demands of a rapidly changing society, or to prepare our students adequately for a productive and satisfying life in the world of today—of *now*.

The alibi of poor financial support, although still valid in many districts, has worn thin. Too many good things are happening in poor districts to place the blame entirely on a lack of sufficient money. As Ianni [1] points out in a portrait of the rebellious suburban student, ". . . that many of them *do* learn and go on to fine colleges does not affirm the school's quality. It is a tribute to their ambitions and aspirations that suburban children learn in spite of their schools."

The Sanctuary Under Attack

One of the most wearisome folk tales of American education is the oft-repeated statement of the middle aged, "If my teacher kept me after school, my father would whip me when I got home."

The implication, of course, is that yesterday's parents al-

---

[1] Francis A. J. Ianni, "Goodbye Mr. Chips?" *Student Unrest: Threat or Promise?* edited by Hart and Saylor (Association for Supervision and Curriculum Development, NEA, 1970), p. 11.

ways sided with the school. Today's teacher probably feels that a complete reversal has taken place. In any event, we cannot ignore the fact that teachers have indeed long enjoyed a comfortable institutionalized sanctuary in matters of craft competency. Except in outstanding instances, teachers have been shielded from accountability by tenure laws and by a profession notoriously willing to close ranks to protect incompetent practitioners. Recent teacher militancy has served to buttress this sanctuary, and both major teachers' organizations have displayed a stubborn reluctance to move into performance evaluation as a basis for a salary differentiation.

Recently, however, powerful forces have begun to attack the defense mechanisms of the educational establishment. Formidable evidence is accumulating that *American students, especially those in urban schools, are simply not learning those things that we say they should learn, and that the fault lies with the schools, not with the students.*

Articulate critics are raising serious questions about our methods and materials, and are even starting to blueprint directions for change. Most significantly, the blueprints are beginning to make sense and the changes have been successfully field tested. Private corporations have created learning laboratories which have been tested with students who have failed to learn in our schools. Payments have been contracted only on demonstrations of success as measured by objective tests. Some results have been positive *and profitable.*

As might have been expected, these intrusions of private enterprise into the business of teaching have been greeted by loud and even angry criticism from teachers' groups. Some of the criticism is entirely justifiable. A certain amount of hoopla and charlatanism seems to creep into much educational innovation, even when it is controlled from within the profession. But it would be a serious mistake to assume that performance contracting can simply be shouted down by teachers and/or administrators. If it is to be defeated, it must be by *equal performance at an equal price* from within our existing schools.

The most painful criticism of our teaching, however, is coming from our older students through their open declarations and in their underground press. When objective educators read and listen to the specific complaints, they show little surprise (except, at times, at the manner of the delivery). They know that our schools have always been organized for convenience and efficiency of operation and that many regulations imposed on students, especially older ones, would not be acceptable to adults. They also realize that the most amazing thing about these regulations is that they have been tolerated so long.

The classroom teacher is in a very strategic position to begin to effect immediate reform simply by accepting the legitimate complaints, correcting conditions in his classroom, and working with others to overcome injustices throughout his school and his district.

Student Complaints

Student criticism of schools throughout America is characterized by a startling uniformity. Where there is so much smoke there *must* be fire. The same items appear over and over again. Perhaps a sample list of "charges" from an affluent suburban school will clarify the basic concerns of students.[2]

Ten Negative and Destructive Aspects of the School System

1. The school system is based on fear.
2. Schools compel students to be dishonest.
3. Teachers force students to give the answers teachers want.
4. The system destroys student eagerness to learn.
5. The school system causes feelings of resentment and alienation on the part of students.
6. Schools foster blind obedience to authority.
7. Self-expression and honest reaction of students are stifled.
8. The school system narrows the scope of ideas.
9. Schools are isolated from new ideas and cultures, thus promoting prejudice.
10. The system promotes self-hate by labelling some students failures before they can prove themselves.

---

[2] "What Happens When Students Criticize?" *Nation's Schools,* Vol. 84, No. 3, September, 1969, p. 59.

The article points out that the above criticism of a suburban district was similar to that published by New York City's High School Student Union about the same time.

The publication of a set of grievances like this always causes controversial reactions, often angry ones. The measurement of each complaint against a given school will vary, of course, but the educator who can recognize no validity in any of them will have an increasingly unhappy experience working in our public schools in the years ahead. The teacher who reads this list and carefully evaluates, in terms of each item, what happens in *his* classroom and in *his* school, will find greater professional satisfaction than the teacher who blindly refutes these complaints as groundless.

Implied Complaints from Our Courts

We must also open our eyes to a new trend in court decisions which substantially parallels the complaints of students. With a long history of defending teachers and schools, our judiciary, especially at the higher levels, is beginning to tell us in unmistakable terms that we are in error.

These court decisions will be considered in Chapter 5, but it is important here to note that many recent decisions have been rendered against the schools on the grounds that we have failed to extend to our students their basic rights and freedom of choice as American citizens. It is perfectly possible that some adults can dismiss the complaints of students on the grounds of immaturity. Can they do the same with our higher courts?

It is possible, of course, to find some comfort in a defensive stance. We can point to significant changes over many years in our better schools. We can even point out inroads of excellence in our poorest schools. It is doubtful, however, if we can make our entire system responsive to the needs of the twenty-first century, unless we abandon the part and begin immediately the painful process of broad-scale reform *which begins in the classroom.*

The Teacher's Attitude

A central consideration in a healthy school is a good classroom climate. The foundation of classroom climate is teacher attitude. Perhaps the single most important contribution to the "how" of teaching was the Golden Rule, *Do unto others as you would have them do unto you.* This sound advice has been vastly ignored. But it has been even more frequently misinterpreted. The verb "do" must be carefully considered. What a teacher *does* to students cannot be solely interpreted by physical actions or spoken words.

Subliminal communications, or "gut reactions," are fully as important as surface communications. Tone of voice, facial expressions, stress on certain words, or even unspoken words can relay strong messages. Identical words of reprimand can communicate thoughtful concern or contemptuous rejection, depending on *how* they are said. *Tolerance is not enough.* The teacher who merely communicates tolerance will not create a sound classroom climate. *Acceptance* is necessary, acceptance of all students by the teacher and by all students of each other. Here we face the problems of the cultural, social class, and generation gaps. The teacher who cherishes middle class values can still accept a student who prefers lower class values. He need not accept the *values,* but he must accept the *student,* as an American citizen with constitutional rights and as a young person whose aspirations can be raised.

A GOOD CLASSROOM CLIMATE

A basic and obvious objective in creating a good classroom climate is to obtain a set of conditions under which optimal learning can take place. It naturally follows that the rights of the individual are not absolute and must be limited by the rights of the group. School discipline has always maintained a firm reference point based on the fact that no student has a right to interfere with the learning opportunities of others. This principle is notably accepted by our courts, for example, in their decisions on hair and clothing styles. When regulations are based on this principle and when punitive action can be reasonably tied to violations thereof, they are generally upheld on appeals. Thus the teacher can begin with this acceptable principle in building his classroom climate.

Now we come to the dangerous step. How does the teacher

The Teacher Works with Militant Youth

apply the principle and, more important, how does he convince the students that it is an acceptable one? Here is where the teacher must refer back to the basic complaints of militant students listed previously and to the negative court rulings of recent years.

One of the contributing factors to today's chaotic youth revolt has probably been the home in which the parents have communicated *no* guiding rationale, *no* creed, *no* sense of direction. This value void, combined with general permissiveness and relative affluence, has set young people adrift like boats without rudders or keels. The development of a positive and democratic classroom climate can provide the keel. The skillful teacher can be the rudder.

Each teacher goes through a series of steps in building and maintaining sound discipline in a good classroom climate. If we begin with the assumption that a teacher accepts the more reasonable complaints of militant students, notes the imperfections in our educational establishment, and recognizes the harsh realities of life outside his classroom walls, perhaps we can suggest a series of steps or phases which will help to create and maintain an optimum classroom climate in our hectic times. Application will vary, of course, with age levels, etc., but in some ways, all of them can be applied in all classrooms.

An example of a reasonable complaint of militant students is the oft-repeated allegation that the school "dehumanizes" the individual. Many petty rules and restrictions exist to contain the foolish behavior of a minority. A teacher can well examine his classroom procedures to see if he, personally, is contributing to this complaint. He can work out, with his students, a modus operandi which allows maximum freedom with minimum interference of teaching and learning.

1. *The Effective Teacher Really Listens to His Students.*

    In the traditional style, the first meeting with any class usually features the teacher telling the students what is expected of them in their academic work and classroom behavior. The same things can be accomplished through a discussion in which the purposes of the year's work, the contractual obligations of the teacher (especially in institutional requirements, such as attendance taking, etc.), and the relevance of the curriculum are all openly and fully discussed. Protesting and demonstrating students can understand, in rational periods, that their protests ought to be directed at the right targets. If law or board policies require certain actions of a teacher and those actions are resented by students, they must direct their protests to the lawmakers and the policymakers—not the teacher.

The teacher points out that the students will participate in all planning, but regulations and activities agreed upon must conform to the basic principle that the rights of the individual must be limited by the rights of the group. The keynote should be an appeal to the sense of fairness of the group in developing procedures which will not violate individual rights nor interfere with the best interests of the group. A reasonable length of time must be devoted to this process. To cut it short in the interests of efficiency would be to revert to the "Here is what I expect of you" approach. Agreements should be put in writing and copies made available to all students.

2. *The Effective Teacher Learns to Know His Students as Individuals.*

Almost every teacher in the world pays lip service to the concept of individual differences and claims to know his students as individuals. Few *really* do. Today, when we are finally beginning to do something institutionally with at least two of the many identifiable differences among students (rate of learning and style of learning), the teacher can no longer merely talk about this vital concept. All teachers, especially elementary teachers, eventually get to know most of their students through a kind of interaction osmosis. The trouble with this is that, for some, it is too little and too late. What about the withdrawn student? Does the teacher ever get to know him when there is little interaction? What about the students who start their patterns of failure on the first day of school? Does it help the teacher to know them as individuals in December?

A secondary teacher may have as many as 150 student contacts daily. It is, perhaps, impractical to study 150 record folders carefully before school starts, but it is possible to start a methodical process of such study. It is also possible to give a priority to students who fail to interact normally.

Questionnaires covering hobbies, interests, and vocational goals can be prepared with relative ease. These will often reveal significant data if read with discrimination. Regular teacher-student conferences and even home visits can supply further information. The experienced teacher knows, of course, that many students consider these questionnaires to be meaningless and fill them in with nonsense. Others fill them in with answers that will please the teacher.

For many years, the average teacher has claimed that he has had no time to do these things. There have been significant changes recently, however, which mandate a new look at the entire business of teaching:

    a. Today students *demand* to be recognized as individuals rather than as faces in a mob. One may not think kindly of *demands* from students, but *there seems to be less inclination each year to invite demonstrations and violence by refusing to heed reasonable demands.*

    b. Teachers' salaries have improved significantly due to their own militancy and demands. While teachers feel they have a long way to go, five things seem clear: (1) the strategy of teachers demanding more money for less work has become more unpopular with school boards; (2) the virtual end of the shortage of teachers will not contribute to further easy and substantial gains; (3) a widespread pattern of reasonable extra pay for extra duties has further improved the teacher's financial position; (4) the need for "moonlighting" during the school year has become less urgent, particularly for veteran teachers; (5) significant further financial gains for classroom teachers will surely be accompanied by firm demands by boards for broader responsibilities. Certainly these would include a greater depth of diagnosis and prescription for the individual child.

If we pursue the comparison popular with teachers, of a physician and a teacher, we must place the doctor in an institution where he sees a great many patients and dispenses prescriptions rapidly after a rather fast examination. The hospital can only afford so many resident physicians. When the hospital agrees to increase its staff and raise the salaries of staff members, it must cut the time given by physicians to functions which can be performed by nurses, aides, orderlies, etc. *It also expects of the physician more thorough individual examination and more careful individual prescription.* This is completely reasonable and proper.

So it is with the teacher. Better salaries and less non-professional duties must result in more thorough individual analyses and better management of differentiated instruction. This may have been a matter of debate ten years ago. It is not today. If individual recognition is not provided for students, violence may result. If not, it is a practical certainty that many of the older ones will walk out the doors and never return. Too many have already done this.

3. *The Effective Teacher Involves His Students in Developing Units and Lessons.*

Once again we seem to be revisiting 1930 progressivism. This time there is a difference. Today's typical student exists in an environment of chaos, crisis, confrontation, and high drama. All the media of communications scream at him constantly. His music of preference is played at full blast and literally injures his ear drums. To use a now older generation expression, everything comes at him like gangbusters. Everything but schools.

Only selective tuning out preserves his sanity. He does his homework with his record player blasting hard rock music. He exists in the midst of an extensive drug culture, which seems to be a crutch for tuning out for many of his peers. With consummate skill he tunes out classroom experiences which, to him, are dull or without meaning in his world. This is the challenge of the teacher of the seventies. *It cannot be met by serving up more of the same.*

Today's teacher must learn to compete with the wildly exciting stimuli of an age of revolution. He must establish relevancy between the experiences in the classroom and the drama in the streets. It must be done thoughtfully. He cannot merely entertain. He cannot simply upstage the media. He must, therefore, involve the student in planning *because the student often is more fully aware of what is going on outside the classroom walls than is the teacher.*

This does not mean that the average student is equipped to create his own curriculum or his own lesson. This does not mean that he is mature enough to distinguish between truth and trivia. Given his choice, he will often opt for entertainment, for kicks. It is up to the teacher to provide guidance in the elusive search for those things which are "most ornamental and most useful." "Time is short and art is long," said Franklin. It is easy to see that "art" is longer today than it was in Franklin's time. Time is certainly shorter if we agree with H. G. Wells that education is in a race with disaster.

The teacher who is seeking student involvement must be aware of a perplexing pitfall that has developed in recent years concerning this matter. The youth rebellion in America has a distaste for formality and form. Parliamentary procedure is only used as a last resort or alternative to complete chaos. Traditional democratic procedures are frowned upon. This is especially evident in high schools today where the traditional Student Council format is rejected by many students. (We should note that this is clearly the fault of faculty advisors and administrators, who have limited its decision making to trivial matters.)

Teachers of younger children may still get by with the old gimmicks, but at the upper levels, the teacher is well advised to consult the students in designing a classroom format for participatory democracy, which is their "thing." It is surprising how well they manage to do this under seemingly chaotic conditions.

It is not necessary to return to the cliché portrait of the progressive classroom where the teacher starts the day with the question, "What shall we learn about today?" Two of the most significant complaints I have heard from students about teaching are: (1) too much repetition of material we already know, and (2) not enough opportunity in our sweeping survey courses to study a smaller segment *in depth*. Why can't these evils be ameliorated? Why not give an extensive examination—say, in an American history course, *before* the year begins? If all the students have mastered segments of the curriculum, why teach it over? If only a few have missed certain other segments, why not single them out for assistance and relieve the others of another repeat? Why not allow every student an opportunity to study something in depth. It means more work for the teacher, but it would be a vast improvement over a sweeping overview of American history, conditioned only (at least in New York State) by the teacher's analysis of past Regents Exams on the subject.

4. *The Effective Teacher Does Not Waive the Rules of Good Teaching.*

While research in learning theory has never had a far-reaching impact on public school practices, it is not fair to condemn the validity of its findings. Learning research has had, comparatively, very inadequate financial support. Then we must face, again, the formidable inertia of the educational establishment. Change comes slowly and painfully in American schools. Change takes time, effort, and faith in the validity of the newer ways. Underpaid and overworked teachers have been less than enthusiastic about making substantial changes in what they do and how they do it.

For the same reasons outlined above for accepting more meaningful student involvement, the excuses for retention of status quo are weakening and the student demands for change are strengthening.

Proper motivation, teaching for transfer, application of theory to reality, accommodation of differing rates and styles of learning, learning in the "marrow bone" through kinesthetic experiences, building the unknown on the known, use of multimedia communications resources, "discovery" methods, and utilizing positive reinforcement are all familiar concepts to good teachers. Under differing names and with no names, these ideas have been known in pedagogy for centuries. They have been so vastly ignored because of: (a) lack of time and resources, and (b) a lack of demand for change from the consuming students.

Times have changed. Teachers *do* have the time. Teachers *do* have the resources. *And the students are no longer accepting the same old routine.* Most particularly among deprived children in the ghettos, we are beginning to see a massive physical resistance to routine mediocrity in the classroom. Even remedial attention when packaged as "more of the same" is failing.

A great deal of recent research has been funded to solve the problem of more effectively teaching disadvantaged students. Exciting discoveries have been made and are recorded in the literature. Much of what is reported, however, is very familiar. Much of the "progressive" rationale has been rediscovered. Perhaps it is reasonable to give to the beginning teacher today a second piece of terse advice to follow as the Golden Rule: *You have learned some rules for good teaching. Do not waive these rules. You cannot get away with it.*

5. *The Effective Teacher Does Not Teach the Curriculum; He Uses the Curriculum to Teach.*

It is my opinion that schools exist to change, to improve society. Without prescribing or espousing specific ideology, our schools work toward the creation of an optimal life style and an optimal material existence for all the people. Schools must be places of trust and truth, where intelligent decision making is taught through a guided tour of the accumulated wisdom of man. Schools should assist the young to seek within themselves the optimal development of their talents and interests to prepare themselves to achieve the best that is in them for service to themselves and their fellowman.

To this end the effective teacher uses all his resources, including the curriculum. Selecting that which serves the student well and rejecting that which fails to serve, he views the curriculum as a means to an end, not an end in itself.

6. *The Effective Teacher Constantly Communicates Higher Academic Expectations, Especially to Disadvantaged Students.*

American public schools have long been enslaved by the I.Q. concept. While it is perfectly true that the *intelligence quotient* has been a handy tool to predict school success, because the tests have generally been designed to do just that, it has also harmed countless students in relegating them to the educational scrap heap.

Teachers must bear in mind *the limitations of intelligence measurement, especially as a predictor of success in the jungle of reality we call life.*

The teacher of yesterday was taught that an I.Q. was constant, that it could not be significantly increased. Today we know this is not true. While the evidence is not all in, there seems to be a general trend of thinking among psychologists that, depending upon environment, significant changes can occur in the I.Q. of a given child. Even a superficial analysis of the effects of ghetto life and racism on a young child would lead to the expectations for success of a seriously disadvantaged student.

The most damning criticism that can be made of American schools is an exposure of the massive and not-so-benign neglect of the student who does not respond well to our teaching. This is, unfortunately, most damning in the case of many teachers who attempt to provide love and acceptance in place of substantial demands for optimum performances.

Love and acceptance are wonderful, of course, especially to the child who has had little or none of these precious commodities. Perhaps love and acceptance are essential as opening steps. The business of the teacher is not merely to make students happy. It is also to provide an atmosphere, an inspiration, and (if necessary) a *demand* that they perform optimally and within their capacity as we know or suspect it. It is far too easy in our public schools for the slow learner to "cop out," to produce less than his potential. He has learned to be cunning, to "con" the teacher by offering acceptable behavior in exchange for a lessening of pressure to do hard work.

The effective teacher will exhaust himself and then find new energy in pulling and pushing the backward student toward intellectual achievements reasonably close to his abilities. This is the most valid demonstration of concern, acceptance, and love that a teacher can exhibit. This is what good teaching is all about.

It seems entirely reasonable to conclude that teaching will become more and more difficult and demanding in the months and years ahead. The teacher will have better resources, which he must learn to use properly. The teacher will receive better financial rewards, *if instruction improves*. The teacher will be a key figure in the channeling of the forces of revolution into positive directions. Most important of all, the teacher will become a powerful agent in the creation of a new world. What more exciting task exists within our society?

> The story of man is the history, first, of the acceptance and imposition of restraints necessary to permit communal life; and second, of the emancipation of the individual within that system of necessary restraints.
>
> **Justice Abe Fortas** [1]

A Contemporary Rationale for School Discipline

AMERICAN DEMOCRATIC TRADITION AS A BASE FOR DISCIPLINE

The bedrock foundation for school discipline is our Constitution. Wherein we have followed its spirit, we have succeeded. Wherein we have failed to follow its spirit, we have failed.

Some years ago I participated in the writing of a book called *Effective Secondary School Discipline* (Larson and Karpas, Prentice-Hall, Inc., 1963). Much of the material in that

---

[1] Abe Fortas, *Concerning Dissent and Civil Disobedience* (New York, New American Library, 1968), p. 59.

book has now been made obsolescent by the youth revolution and other contemporary events. I would like to quote, however, a set of principles which has not been outmoded by current events.

Principles of Secondary School Discipline

1. Disciplinary policies should be in harmony with the total goals of education.

The disciplinary procedures of a school should never be permitted to become an end in themselves, nor be confused with procedures necessary in other types of institutions. The first criterion for any secondary school disciplinary procedure should be the question, "Is this a sound educational practice?"

2. Disciplinary policies should be in harmony with the teachings of science; notably psychology and sociology.

3. Disciplinary policies should be in harmony with the principles of a democratic society; i.e., equal justice for all, respect for the rights and dignity of the individual, humanitarian treatment for all.

4. Disciplinary policies should stress the *responsibilities* as well as the rights of an individual.

5. Disciplinary policies should be positive and directed to the goal of *self-discipline*. The emphasis should be on the benefits to the group and the individual of good self-discipline rather than on punitive measures.

6. Disciplinary policies should be primarily preventive, secondarily corrective, and never retributive.

I resubmit the above list on the basis that while our schools should work toward changing society for the betterment of man, they are also instruments of our national government, regulated by our states and located in our towns and cities within their non-sectarian and non-political framework, and they must serve the major purposes of our democracy as stated in our Constitution and as interpreted by our courts. Above all, their major function is to provide *education* for all American youth not better served by another type of institution. All personnel in our schools, all regulatory machinery of the schools, all procedures, all structures and hardware must be measured in the last analysis by how well or how badly they serve that major purpose. This has become vividly clear in recent years when many court decisions involving student behavior, dress, haircuts, etc. seem to be based on the question, "Does it interfere with education?"

When American schools serve the purpose of perpetuating American democracy, they are not perpetuating a static way of life. Our traditions are dynamic, our Constitution flexible enough to accommodate change. Where we have failed our youth is in neglecting to extend to them their rights under the Constitution. Where their own radical leaders are failing them is in similar denials of Constitutional rights; notably, in denying freedom of speech to those whose viewpoint is "incorrect" in the opinion of those leaders.

Our schools must also be dynamic and become flexible enough to serve the needs of today and tomorrow. This does *not* mean that we must swivel like a weather vane to every vagrant breeze. It does *not* mean that we must surrender to every noisy minority group. It does *not* mean that we should abandon our basic notion that the rights of the individual must be contained by the rights of the group.

LAW AS A BASE FOR DISCIPLINE

The school exists within a framework of law at three levels: federal, state, and local. Usually the most rigid laws restricting the choices of school officials are the state laws. Some are good, many are superfluous and/or anachronistic, and some are very bad. The school board and its employees have no right to select the laws they wish to obey. They must obey and enforce them all. They have, of course, all the rights of citizens to work legally to change bad laws; but until these laws are changed, repealed, or declared unconstitutional, they must be enforced.

Young people are less patient with bad laws. They often feel that these laws should be broken and they do not always choose the methods of Thoreau and Ghandi to break them. They have turned too often to violence. Here is where they clash with authority figures, who take the position that peaceful protest and the electoral process are the only valid instruments to combat bad laws in a free society.

In spite of the many inequities in our society and our American system, it can be reasonably stated that no people anywhere or at any time enjoyed the degree of freedom of expression and action enjoyed now by the American people. Even children in school are protected by the rights of American citizenship under the Constitution.

What Happened to "in loco parentis?"

Until very recently, school discipline has been based on a general agreement in our society that the teacher was acting in place of the parent and was entitled to do anything that a *reasonable* parent would do. The courts only overruled educators who demonstrated cruelty or capriciousness in punishment. This has now been significantly modified by court decisions, which have extended all the rights of the Constitution, especially *Due Process of Law* to the student in school, while parents are still limited only by laws pertaining to cruelty in its various manifestations.

The Schools Still Have Legal Responsibilities

Certain responsibilities are spelled out for the schools and their administrators, especially in state laws. In some cases, school board members are held individually financially responsible when laws are not properly obeyed (as in the Pennsylvania "surcharge" law). In all states, teachers, principals, and superintendents have specific legal obligations.

In 1969, a Maryland elementary teacher left her classroom for a few minutes during an exercise period. As a result of an accidental fall, a student broke two front teeth. A judge ordered the teacher to pay the parents $6,131, citing a ruling by a New York judge who stated,[2] "Parents do not send their children to school to be returned to them maimed because of the absence of proper supervision."

Due process of law, in terms of school discipline, is simply protection against punishment by whim. It guarantees the student a definite procedure which protects his individual rights

---

[2] "Education, U.S.A.," a weekly report on Educational Affairs, National School Public Relations Association, Washington, D.C., March 3, 1969.

against arbitrary exercise of authority, just as the Constitution guarantees any citizen a fair trial. This should be no problem for educators.

There has been a great deal of concern and frustration exhibited by educators over these rulings, but a careful overview of the more important decisions reveals no major cause for alarm. As long as the schools have been reasonable and fair, they have been upheld by the courts. Legal procedures and representation by counsel must be offered only where serious consequences to students, such as expulsion or confinement, may be involved.

The evidence of rulings and opinions quoted in recent literature seems to indicate that we do not have to establish full-fledged courts of law within our schools. Quasi-legal procedures are only necessary when the consequences of an act by a student can lead to serious consequences, such as assignment to a correctional institution or lengthy suspension from school. No student has a right to be represented by an attorney if he is seen throwing a spitball. On the other hand, the school should be certain that he did, indeed, throw the spitball before assigning punishment.

Excursions into style setting, however, such as clothing and hair regulations, are not being uniformly upheld unless the school proves that the offender's taste interferes with the educative process. Extremely bizarre or indecent clothing would obviously distract attention in the classroom. It has become apparent that the problem of hair and clothing regulations is very popular with the press. This was especially true in the early sixties, when these regulations were generally being upheld by the courts in their sometimes arbitrary decisions in this area. Some of the efforts were downright silly, especially the frantic battle of administrators against the mini-skirt.

In defense of our embattled secondary administrators, however, it must be noted that every high school has a certain number of students who will push any regulation to its limit and resort to wild extremes of bad taste in the absence of any regulations. High school styles are still considered good copy for humorous pieces that cast the principal as a puritanical and outmoded villain fighting against forces of progress. While this may or may not annoy this much harassed official, he *knows* what is expected of him under law and school policies. He must exercise his judgment in each case to prevent hair and clothing styles from interfering with the process of education. This is *all* he is permitted to do and it is a tough job. I have no magic formula to help him.

The principle of "reasonable supervision" is still very much with us even though school boards are largely immune from damage suits. Teachers and administrators must bear this in mind when high school students demand or request freedom from adult supervision in certain school activities. In these cases, their protests should be redirected to the state legislature and/or the courts.

Channeling Student Militancy

Too often, student militants strike out blindly at "The Establishment" without critical analyses of the actual centers of power. The school administrator who is attacked for the Indo-China war, polluted air, etc. has reason for his frustration and anger. Why should he be made accountable for situations which he did not create and over which he has no control beyond that of a citizen of the republic? When a state law prevents the granting of a student request, it is no longer sufficient simply to tell him so. If, however, a committee of student leaders can be *shown* the law and perhaps even have it explained by an attorney, their inherent sense of fairness will very likely redirect their thrust into the proper direction. Perhaps the request will be withdrawn. In any event, it will narrow the issues down to those over which the school has the right to make decisions. This is a step in the right direction.

HUMANITARIAN AND PRAGMATIC BASES FOR DISCIPLINE

Law and order have become trigger words in the youth rebellion, and have also become associated with heavy-handed police action in some instances. *Justice* is a preferred retort today. While the elders in our society equate law and justice, young people do not. They point to unjust laws such as the former segregation laws. They point to interpretations of laws and selective enforcement of them and cite the evidence that capital punishment laws and draft laws have often favored the wealthy and white segments of our society. While vast improvements have been made in recent years, we must bear this bit of history firmly in mind as we create and administer the machinery of justice in our schools.

Most young people have no difficulty with the concept of authority. They do resent *authoritarianism*. Operating with large numbers of students, many of whom are immature, some of whom are alienated from society, and a few of whom are emotionally disturbed or simply young criminals, public schools have had to build a formidable structure of rules and regulations, most of which were created expressly to contain the troublesome minority. It is little wonder that they annoy the law-abiding majority.

To administer this massive hodge-podge of sometimes petty rules, justice machinery was created to handle great numbers of minor and major infractions as efficiently and as quickly as possible so that the schools could get on with the basic business of teaching. It is understandable that "due process" sometimes has suffered. School administrators work with young people whose sense of fairness has been as much outraged when a student "gets away" with an infraction as when an innocent receives minor punishment. Thus, the justice machinery attempts to weave a tight net that sometimes scoops up the innocent. The most glaring example of this, of course, is that teacher who detains an entire class after school because she could not identify the monster who threw an eraser.

Now students are demanding a better justice machine which will not ensnare the innocent, even for minor offenses involving minor punishment. One wonders if there is a model in the world of such judicial excellence. It can certainly not be found in the courts of our land today, particularly not in our criminal courts.

In a feature article in *Life Magazine* of August 7, 1970, writer Dale Wittner painted a gloomy portrait of mismanaged and overtaxed courts in which the odds heavily favored the hardened criminal going unpunished, over and over again. He states that, "So strained, so clogged with humanity have they (the courts) become, that substantial justice is only an occasional, almost accidental product."

Is it not strange that no major segment of the youth rebellion has selected our entire judicial system as a target for protest, and have been content to object only in instances when radical leaders have been tried? It is ironic but understandable (because of the relative seriousness of offenses and punishments) that adult courts seem to choose to err in the direction of letting offenders go free, while school disciplinarians seem to prefer a tighter system that sometimes ensnares the innocent in its zeal to catch up with all the guilty.

Let us consider now a reasonable approach to contemporary discipline problems in the schools, beginning with a basic foundation in law as interpreted today and moving on to specific current phenomena. Following this, the next chapter will concentrate on the machinery of discipline and the prevention and containment of violence in our schools.

AUTHORITY WITHOUT AUTHORITARIANISM

Reformers and revolutionaries, under our Constitution, may advocate change—be it ever so radical. They may even organize to achieve that change. (e.g. The American Nazi Party and The American Communist Party). They may demonstrate if they break no laws. *But they may not break any laws in carrying out their programs.*

Even "bad" laws must be obeyed, and the highest ideals invoked in breaking them cannot protect the violator from punishment. Since these Constitutional rights are now clearly extended to students of any age, in considering the various forms of student dissent, school administrators must proceed with these principles firmly in mind. It is further helpful, however, to separate two basic methods of breaking an unpopular law: peaceful civil disobedience as practiced by Thoreau, Ghandi, King, et al and violence as practiced by various radical youth organizations. The following guidelines have been developed out of the experience of administrators, including the author,

A Contemporary Rationale for School Discipline

who have faced various forms of student dissent including violence and riots.

- Protest and radical proposals are not *per se* against the law. But if protest interferes with education, it must be (in order of preference) redirected or stopped. If laws of slander, trespassing, assault, etc. are broken, the protest must be stopped.
- Peaceful civil disobedience can be handled by the school administration, but when *any* laws are broken, the violators should be turned over to the police and complaints should be filed by appropriate persons.
- Violence, unless it is extremely limited and easily stopped by school personnel, should be referred to the police as quickly as possible. When violence is anticipated, the police should be informed.

Freedom of Expression

There are, and always will be, limitations on freedom of speech. They are basically simple and can be taught to students, especially secondary students. Generally speaking, these limitations are based on the rights of others. When free speech endangers another person (shouting "fire" in a crowded theatre, inciting to riot under dangerous circumstances, etc.), *it is not legal, not moral, not right.*

When free speech interferes with the rights and privileges of others (blocking a highway, obstructing or "occupying" spaces used for work, etc.), *it is not legal, not moral, not right.*

When free speech slanders another person, it is subject to the laws of libel and slander. Freedom of expression, then, is not an absolute. It is subject to several conditions.

The Underground Press

One of the more popular fads of the youth movement is the publication of underground newspapers. Usually ineptly produced, most of them die rather quickly (if they are ignored) because the organizers run out of: (a) significant things to say, (b) writing talent, (c) interested readers, (d) money and other resources, (e) energy. When they are crushed and martyred, they gain a new lease on life, depending upon the extent and degree of repression. Often they linger on simply because they have been crushed.

When supported by radical segments of older youth, however, or when they are regionalized as in the secondary schools of a large city, they can become dangerous in their tendencies to incite violence.

Usually underground publications are born because official student publications are inadequate and/or heavily controlled by teachers or administrators. The basic problem is that *without competent technical advice* the young publishers turn out quite bad work. They are hardly ever aware of the laws concerning slander, obscenity, and invasion of privacy which govern all publications. They drearily imitate the style and format of avant-garde college publications. Worst of all, they seldom know how to research a story and how to come up with simple truth. For these reasons, they cause more anger and frustration among administrators and teachers than they deserve.

The first step to take is to eliminate reasons for their existence. This can be done by providing a high quality school publication (or publications), adequately advised, *with a minimum of censorship,* and *frequently published.* Invite the paper to criticize, but see that it thoroughly researches its crusades. See that all segments of student opinion may be published. See that it complies to laws which govern commercial papers. See that it is adequately supported.

When underground papers do appear, try to ignore them unless they break the law or interfere with the educative process. If they criticize the school and are within the bounds of reason and truth, grin and bear it. One way of "listening" to students is to read their prose with an open mind.

In many cases, particularly where unofficial papers have failed, the official paper has benefitted by inviting the underground journalists to join its staff. Freedom from oppressive censorship and awareness of press law can be excellent training for a youngster who wants to express himself in writing. Attention seeking through pure sensationalism does not sustain lengthy satisfaction for intelligent kids.

A Contemporary Rationale for School Discipline

Wearing Buttons

Wearing buttons as a form of freedom of expression has been adjudicated as a right of students under the First Amendment. They are, however, subject to the same legal restraints as any form of free speech in the schools. Students cannot *force* other students to wear or not wear legal buttons. The buttons cannot interfere with education. They cannot slander groups or individuals. They cannot contain inflammatory words which could lead to violence. They cannot be obscene.

The last item can be tricky. Some of the slogans are extremely sophisticated and require a high degree of sophistication for one to understand the double meaning. Others really can be interpreted several ways. What about "Make love not war."? The young claim that this refers to spiritual love and that only the word "war" is obscene. Perhaps the principal should confiscate the button on the grounds that the wearer admitted that it contained an obscene word—"war." Who knows?

Acts of Symbolism

One of the heartbreaking symptoms of the youth rebellion is the conscious and growing aversion to patriotism. Student activists, at the time of this writing, have even permitted right wing groups to monopolize the symbolism of the American flag. To the aging liberal who loves his land and refuses to permit any group to preempt the flag for its purposes, this is a trend that is difficult to understand.

It has been pointed out repeatedly that nationalism is thriving in pre-industrial countries and that it is dying in post-industrial countries. If the young were merely reacting against the cheap jingoism that so often passes for patriotism, the tasteless use of the spirit of the fatherland to promote patent ideologies or even patent medicine, the association of the flag with status quo, it would be easier to understand. No serious attempts are even being made by the young to substitute internationalism for nationalism. It seems to the elders that the young are completely rejecting their land as being beyond redemption. This rejection takes a variety of forms, and perhaps we had better curb our anger and frustration to ask ourselves a few searching questions:

1. Have we done an *intelligent* job of teaching our children to love their country?
2. Have we extended ourselves to promote *effective* programs to honor national holidays or have we simply invited any "speaker" who was eager to appear?
3. Have we taught our children the meaning of the pledge of allegiance or have we taught them the meaning of the *words?* Try this: call together at random five or six secondary students from any school anywhere. Ask each one if he can recall being taught the *meaning* of the flag ceremony. Then ask him for his interpretation.

The Compulsory Flag Salute

Most states have laws permitting or requiring the flag salute of all students. Since 1944, however, a Supreme Court ruling has exempted those who refuse to do so "for religious reasons."

In 1969, however, three students were suspended in New York City for refusing to salute the flag or stand during the pledge or leave the room during the ceremony. One objected to the words "under God," claiming a belief in atheism. The other stated that the words "with liberty and justice for all" were false today.

The U.S. District Court ruled against the school system, noting that students who refuse to participate "for reasons of conscience" should not be treated in any different way from those who participate.

Until this matter is settled by the Supreme Court, it would be advisable to proceed with caution. I strongly recommend, however, that every school and every school district survey its policies, regulations, and curriculum to determine whether a healthy, intelligent, and effective effort is being made to teach youngsters to honor and love their country.

Desecrating the Flag

Proper usage of the American flag is thoroughly covered by law. The law must be enforced. Lower courts have upheld these laws, but they have not yet been ruled upon in terms of the Constitution by the Supreme Court. One must bear in mind, however, that burning is a method prescribed by law for disposing of a worn or soiled flag. The demonstrator who burns a flag in protest and is arrested, may claim that he is legally disposing of a worn-out flag.

So much for technicalities. The disturbing element here is that students turn to this form of iconoclasm and, in so doing, surrender the flag, conceding it to be a symbol of special groups whom they despise. They know that disrespect to the flag arouses wrath among their elders and they delight in any act that "blows their minds." What they seem to fail to comprehend is that it is *their* flag they dishonor. It represents *their* freedom of expression. It represents *them,* and they are dishonoring themselves.

Perhaps we should make this clear in our classrooms. We could begin with a reading of the law in respect to what can and cannot be done with the American flag. Then we should administratively enforce the law. Here, again, we must rely on common sense and good judgment. It would be difficult to prove that a flag worn on the sleeve of a jacket, even though the intent is to display cynicism, breaks the law. A flag worn on the seat of the trousers is another matter. The student should be asked to remove it. If he fails to comply, he should become involved in a parental interview in which the law is explained. If he still fails to comply, he should be suspended. I cannot believe that any school official would be overruled by a court in a case like that.

Personal Appearance

Until 1969, the lower courts had generally sustained principals in regulations which limited the length of boys' hair. This trend was reversed, however, in 1969 following a ruling in Wisconsin based on the Fourteenth Amendment and, at the same time, a ruling of the Supreme Court permitting the wearing of black armbands. Two principles became clear: (1) students are protected by the Constitution, even in schools; (2) their rights cannot be denied them because administrators anticipate disturbances or distractions as a result of exercising those rights.

Basically, our courts have taken the position that school teachers, administrators, or boards have no business dictating fashions in clothing or hair style. Such regulations would violate the Fourteenth Amendment *except where:*

1. A student's health is involved, such as in wearing clothing inappropriate to weather and climate.

2. A student's safety is involved, such as in shop, gym, or home economics activities.
3. The hair or clothing style selected interferes with the educative process, and the school can reasonably prove this.

These rulings also indirectly affect teachers, who are no longer expected to wear clothing patterned after the styles preferred by the most conservative elements of the community. When extreme costumery interferes with education, however, the administration can require change.

Behavior Codes

It seems clear that all school regulations which are older than a few years, ought to be reviewed in the light of recent court decisions, and especially the principle of due process of law.

Student participation in the formulation of a new code seems, at this time, almost essential. Ideally, teachers, administrators, the school board, and parents should be involved. Before adoption, the entire code should be reviewed by an attorney.

Certain restrictions on behavior are necessary for the health, safety, and welfare of students and can be upheld in any court in the land. Silence in libraries and study areas, for example, will always be an essential condition for good education. Reasonable rules of procedure and conduct in cafeterias, auditoriums, shops, laboratories, corridors, and school buses are absolutely necessary. Smoking is now clearly a health hazard. Certain principles should be used as criteria in developing these codes:

1. Behavior controls should be based on the health, safety, and welfare of all and prescribe conditions essential to the effective pursuit of the educative process.
2. Behavior controls should be broad and indicate reasons for their existence; for example: "Due to the health hazards documented by the Surgeon General of the United States and safety hazards indicated in City Fire Regulations, smoking will not be permitted in the _____ School or on the School Grounds." Petty and silly "Don't spit on the floor" rules should be avoided.
3. Behavior controls should not limit or deny the Constitutional

A Contemporary Rationale for School Discipline

rights of any individual, unless the exercise of any of those rights interferes with education or threatens the health, safety, or welfare of other individuals.
4. Behavioral controls should apply to all students.
5. Within the limitations of the unique problems of a given building, behavioral controls at a given level (secondary or elementary, for example) should be consistent throughout a school district.
6. Every student, teacher, and administrator should be provided with a copy of the code. (It would not be a bad idea to send copies to parents.)

Suspension and Expulsion

The common practice of suspending students for a short period of time in order to force a parent conference needs no defense, educationally or legally, unless it is overused or utilized in trivial cases. The administrator needs a couple of days to gather current data in order to conduct an intelligent conference. There is no point to inconveniencing a parent in this manner merely to discuss whether or not Johnny pulled Mary's hair. Much may be gained, however, from a discussion of Johnny's *total behavior* in school and his general attitude. It is a valid cliché that it is difficult to see the parents of students who can profit most from a school-home partnership. The short suspension, used in this manner, can benefit everyone.

Used merely as punishment, however, it is open to question. Some troublesome students like to stay out of school. Some of the most troublesome ones are annoyed at being isolated from their friends and "the action."

Lengthy and permanent suspension and expulsion, however, is another matter. Here "due process" had better be evident, including the right of representation by an attorney.

It is most significant to note at this point that once due process of law has been provided, *the action of the school does not have to be evaluated on the basis of the single infraction which may have precipitated the expulsion.* This is most important. If a student's pattern of behavior indicates a "clear and present" danger or clearly interferes with the education of others, he may (depending upon state laws) be expelled by the district. In some states, this action can only be taken by a school board. In others, the administration has the authority.

In 1969, in New York State, a student was implicated in a bomb scare but was found innocent. *Based on his past record,* however, he was suspended for six months. In an appeal to the State Commissioner, *the superintendent was upheld in his right to suspend a student for general reasons.*

This may or may not be acceptable as a precedent in other states, but it is most significant to note this basic difference between judicial procedures in school and in an adult court.

The best procedure to follow today in cases of permanent or lengthy expulsion is to hold a formal (but not public) hearing before the board, in which the defendent is permitted representation by an attorney and the district is represented by its attorney, who may act as prosecutor. All witnesses should be heard fully with as little reliance as possible on usual courtroom procedural rules or relevance, hearsay, etc. If possible, a court stenographer should record the proceedings in case of appeals. In that way, there will be no problem with "due process."

It is assumed, of course, that the parents are first given an opportunity to withdraw the student voluntarily.

Corporal Punishment

Perhaps too many words have already been written on this subject. It is, of course, always necessary to distinguish carefully between the use of force and the use of corporal punishment. Sometimes this is difficult to do in the lower elementary grades. Attitudes toward the use of hands by teachers vary greatly in different parts of our nation. Each teacher, in reference to the use of force, must examine his conscience *and* the laws and regulations of his district and state.

In working with young children, some teachers feel that it is necessary to use appropriate force when necessary, even a mild slap on the wrist or derriere once in a while. Having had no experience with teaching large numbers of very young children, I defer to their judgment. I would warn seriously, however, against the use of force in anger where it can become excessive. Courts take a dim view of excessive force, and there are enough legal precedents available to state flatly that no student should ever, under any circumstances be struck anywhere on his head.

I feel strongly that corporal punishment at the secondary level is, among other things, a waste of time and effort. It has been my observation over the years that the very worst problem boys in secondary schools have received the most corporal punishment at home. It has failed there and will fail in the school.

State laws and local regulations frequently are silent on the subject of corporal punishment, thereby permitting it. Courts have, in the past, generally backed teachers in the use of corporal punishment, providing it was administered with reason. We all know now, however, that the scene has changed. Our higher courts are showing a great concern for the rights of the individual student. I would advise teachers to avoid using force, except where it is necessary for self-defense or to prevent a dangerous situation which would threaten injury to others.

6

> Young people today are extremely sensitive to distinctions between authority and authoritarianism, between necessary authority and naked power, between justice and order. We had best be aware of this as we design new machinery of governance.
>
> **Knute Larson**

Maintaining Justice, Law, and Order in the School

THE MACHINERY OF JUSTICE

It is impossible to understand the organizational needs of any public school without first knowing that the principal and his staff are expected, under law, to assume a primary responsibility for the safety, health, and well-being of all students while they are in attendance. Court decisions over the years have made this extremely clear. Regardless of the type of organization invoked for instruction, regardless of the philosophy of education followed, regardless of the methods used in teaching, *reasonable supervision* must be enforced or school personnel are liable for negligence if a student is injured in any way.

Maintaining Justice, Law, and Order in the School

When a home economics teacher sends two girls to a nearby store for a pound of sugar, the *teacher* is responsible for their safety. If the principal has approved the trip, *he* is responsible. When racial incidents result in massive physical disorder, the principal's choice of decisions is fairly limited. Close school? Call the police? Assign teachers to solve the problem? Whatever he does, it must be based on the moral and legal certainty that his basic responsibility is for the safety and welfare of all his students. The courts have made decision after decision underscoring the simple idea that parents are entitled to send their children to school with a reasonable certainty that they will not return injured—physically or psychologically.

In the well-organized schools of the past, *all* teachers shared this responsibility for *all* students at *all* times. Regardless of what major changes must take place in our schools (and they *must*), this is one tradition which cannot be abandoned. There is nothing in its preservation which precludes the possibility of far more independent work being pursued on or off campus. As a matter of fact, the major failures of off-campus study in our high schools have taken place where little or no thought was given to this principle. Students who are ready for freedom of action should have it. Students who are not ready should not have it. If parents are involved in the decision making, there should be no great problem involved.

Unfortunately, as our schools become more involved in the varied manifestations of revolt, there is a tendency among many teachers to circumscribe their responsibilities, to ignore bad behavior in corridors, to see and hear selectively as they move around a building, to take notice of students only in areas to which they have been specifically assigned. More and more teachers' contracts include non-professional aides for this type of work. A dangerous trend is visible. While it is perfectly true that teachers should be relieved of non-professional chores, it is not true that the responsibility for supervision of students in large-group settings is a non-professional function. The supervision may, of course, be assisted by aides, but an experienced teacher must be in charge. School cafeterias are not prison cafeterias. Experienced teachers know the precise amount of tension release and informality necessary in a lunchroom—non-professionals do not. Teachers cannot abandon their overall responsibility for the behavioral tone of a school. It simply will not work, unless we knowingly agree that our schools should become prisons. Some students feel that they are prisons now.

The ordinary machinery of school discipline is too familiar to bear description here. Solidly based on the goal of preserving order through behavioral restraints and on backing the teachers, the system has disadvantages, especially for students. In minor matters, guilt is often assumed in cases of doubt. Basically, the student with a record of past offenses is considered guilty until he proves his innocence. The reverse is often true of the student with a good record. The disciplinary official is caught in a bind. Although he does not conceive of his function as that of an executioner, he knows that teachers have to be backed in discipline. When a student insists on his innocence in a minor matter, the disciplinarian follows a familiar line: "Perhaps the teacher made an honest mistake. What of it? Don't you make mistakes? Serving detention for one night won't kill you. How about all the times you were guilty and didn't get caught? It all balances out."

The amazing thing is that this system has worked reasonably well. Part of the reason for this is the basic benevolence with which most schools administer petty injustice. Part of it is due to the patience and good common sense of students. But it must also be mentioned that in the subculture of secondary students, a clean disciplinary record is not always regarded as a positive recommendation for being acceptable to the group.

The system breaks down when arbitrary judgments result in injustice in serious cases. In any event, the day of tyranny, minor or major, is coming to an end in school discipline. Not only have the students lost their patience, but our Supreme Court has mandated "due process of law" even for children in school.

Schools are now faced with a problem of adjustment. Teachers must still be backed in discipline. Conditions conducive to effective learning must still be maintained. All this must be accomplished under due process of law and without having our educational operations bogged down in a massive, slow-moving stream of petty disciplinary hearings.

Maintaining Justice, Law, and Order in the School

A desire for or a mandate for change in any school always seems to set in motion the same responses and conclusions. The first step is *always* to appoint a committee. After the committee and coffee start, school people always recommend the addition of more personnel. Only when this recommendation is flatly denied, may we suggest the more effective use of existing personnel.

It might also be mentioned that the mere addition of another disciplinary administrator would probably provide more of the same when what is needed is more of *something different*. Nor is there any assurance that adding another administrator might not merely mean that the same administrative operation pattern will be conducted in a more leisurely manner. Let us turn to some specific possibilities for the better use of existing personnel.

Using Teachers

Many secondary schools and some elementary schools utilize teachers in discipline councils. As a group, these teachers advise principals on discipline policies and procedures. As individuals, they often process minor infractions. This can be a rewarding experience, both to the teacher who wishes to remain a teacher and to the teacher who aspires to administration. Compensation may be provided in extra pay, freedom from other non-teaching duties, or (in secondary schools) partial relief from class loads. I have seen this method used very successfully in larger secondary schools.

Using Counselors

Professional guidance workers have for decades maintained a stance that no counselor can be involved in discipline. In my opinion, this rigid line is too simplistic. While it may be true that no counselor should be required to hand out punishment (even though good parents are able to counsel *and* punish equally effectively), it does seem obvious that a counselor should have a key role in preventive discipline or, if one prefers, the prevention of discipline.

I feel that a good disciplinarian is also a good counselor. For years I have witnessed the return of the graduates and dropouts who were constantly in trouble, to visit the schools. Often they seek out first their discipline administrators, their principals, and *their strictest teachers*. Their surface reason seems to be to demonstrate that they have become good citizens. I feel that an underlying reason is to pay respect to those who punished them with justice and compassion when they were wrong.

Guidance people, working with classroom teachers, should develop guidelines for *priority referrals* of students to their counselors. Technically this now takes place in practically all schools. Actually it really takes place in very few schools. Poor communications between teachers and counselors is usually the reason for this. Today, as never before, there is an urgent need to stress the importance of *preventive discipline*. This is clearly a primary concern of guidance. It is curious that this function seems to be growing in the elementary schools where formal guidance programs are in a very early stage of development. A cynic might observe that the right thing is happening for the wrong reason; i.e., the overburdened elementary principal who has no assistant turns over these responsibilities to the newly appointed elementary counselor. Be that as it may, elementary guidance counselors seem to be moving in the right direction.

Using Department Heads

I offer no apology for using the archaic designation for the secondary school teachers who have been assigned the chief responsibility for instruction and curriculum within given academic disciplines. I have no quarrel with the current trend of breaking the barriers between the traditional disciplines, or of combining material in new packages involving inter-disciplinary coordination. I merely wish at this point to remind the reader of the true cliché, that much discipline trouble is traceable to poor curriculum and poor teaching. In any secondary school of any size and in the elementary schools under differing titles, are professionals whose chief concern is with these central functions of our schools. In my opinion, they are improving discipline by improving learning; but I also feel that they can function very effectively as troubleshooters. When, for example, a disciplinary official interviews a student whose trouble stems from his relationship with a teacher whose methods or materials can be questioned, what more logical avenue of referral could be available than the person to whom that teacher turns for assistance in these matters? This valuable and logical avenue of referral has been much neglected in the past. I have seen the removal of an inept teacher or the improvement of such a teacher result in a significant drop in disciplinary referrals. There is simply no question about the relationship between good behavior and good teaching. Why not involve instructional leaders directly in the process of discipline?

Using Students

When everything else fails, we turn to students for help. Why not turn to them *before* everything else fails. Many hasty efforts are being made today to involve students, especially at the secondary levels, in disciplinary procedures. Most of these projects utilize students in advisory roles in the overhaul of policies and regulations. The practice seems to succeed best where it is used *honestly,* where something actually *happens* as a result of student recommendations. Many student ideas will be impractical, of course, and many will collide with board policies or with laws. On the other hand, it is not wise to reject an idea simply because it has been tried without success previously. There is a season for all things. In the proper season, yesterday's bad idea can become today's stroke of genius.

Students today differ from students of the past in many significant ways. Not the least of these is their deeply embedded desire to reform inadequate institutions of society. It may well be time, for example, to take down from the attic of secondary education the long-discarded *student court,* dust it off, and take a new look at it.

Why couldn't an intelligently guided student court assist the administration with minor offenses, especially in high schools? Most student courts of several decades ago failed because participating students were given little or no preparation or guidance. Typically, they assigned punishment that was *too severe* for the offense. Who knows what today's students would do with an intelligently constructed judicial procedure in which they played a realistic part?

Undoubtedly there are American schools in which this revival has taken place or in which student courts have persisted through the years. Very little useful descriptive material seems to be available in the professional literature.

Many types of student organizations are becoming involved in various phases of discipline today. In schools serving minority groups, *intergroup councils* are developing to improve relationships between racial groups. Quite often these councils serve the purpose of averting injustice when a student can turn to this channel for appeal or clarification when he feels the Establishment has been unfair. This type of organization, along with a student court or any other student group concerned with discipline (as well as teacher groups), must work very closely with the principal, and especially with the administrator whose chief assignment involves the machinery of discipline.

However the machinery is designed to administer justice in the school, a primary concern must be with the best possible lines of communication among parents, students, teachers, faculty, and administrators. Experience teaches us that the most effective means of communication occurs face to face. Principals have always been haunted by the knowledge that they do not have enough time to get out of the office to talk with students and teachers. Today the desk-bound principal is *really* asking for trouble!

An interesting example of face-to-face involvement of the major segments of a secondary school is in the Student, Faculty Administrative Council of the Ramapo (New York State) Regional High School, described briefly in *Parade Magazine* of the *Philadelphia Sunday Bulletin* of May 3, 1970.

This Council was conceived in desperation and was created to meet the needs of a near chaotic situation. The district vested in this Council the authority to determine the direction of school policies and procedures with *no veto power to be retained by the principal*. The latter voluntarily surrendered this power and retained only one vote on the Council. The only restraints on the Council are laws and policies. This article, supplemented by my own investigation, reveals that the decisions made by this Council have followed the same common-sense approach taken by any enlightened and competent school administration.

In this case, the faculty and the school board approved the abdication of powers by the principal in a crisis situation. While

I would seriously question the legality or wisdom of such a move under ordinary circumstances or as a permanent modus operandi, it did help to resolve a serious problem. I feel, however, that enlightened administration can achieve the same goals in most schools by preventive measures which are based on a serious consideration of the grievances of students today. The pattern of complaints about our schools, and especially about their administration of discipline, is so amazingly similar throughout our nation (and even the world) that it is virtually impossible not to see the handwriting on the wall. We must make significant changes and we must do it soon. The choice is no longer ours.

THE ENFORCEMENT OF LAW

I have indicated the obvious in pointing out that our actions are circumscribed by law and district policies. What we must remember, however, is that local laws and school board policies, which are a form of law, can be changed very quickly. Preventive medicine is also indicated here. Instead of waiting until a crisis reveals the inadequacy of a policy, it would be wise to study all existing policies to see if they are still relevant *or even legal* anymore. Recent court interpretations (flag salute requirements, for example) have made many school policies and regulations illegal. The time to update them is *before* the crisis reveals their obsolescence.

Under ordinary conditions and in ordinary times, it is not considered wise for school boards to create *anticipatory* policies or regulations. The first time a given problem arises it is dealt with *ad hoc,* with the combined wisdom of the board and the advice of the superintendent. Then this action is translated into policy and/or regulatory language to ensure similar actions in the future.

We are not living in normal times, however. Changes happen swiftly and they can often be predicted. The district which has no significant drug problem should not hesitate to prepare an intelligent drug policy in these times. The failure to *anticipate* trouble today can be as catastrophic as the failure of a seaside community to anticipate a hurricane when warnings have been broadcast.

Working with the Police

If school people feel that their problems are nearly insurmountable today, they may find some small comfort in examining the plight of the police. Understaffed, undersupported, often subject to general abuse and contempt by segments of the *adult* community, our police are hemmed in today by laws and court decisions that make their work very difficult. Student extremists have declared war on *all* police. Labelling them *pigs*, they blindly classify every law enforcement officer as an enemy. We must face the seriousness of this situation when signs appear on our prestige campuses urging "KILL THE PIGS." Fanaticism? Yes, but we must be deeply concerned with the fact that the spill-over of this attitude has developed varying stages of negative attitudes toward the police in an enormous segment of our responsible youth population. There is direct and indisputable evidence of police brutality which youngsters find hard to ignore. There is direct and indisputable evidence of unspeakable provocation of police by young activists, many of whom deliberately seek physical confrontation. Millions of television viewers have seen both sides of the situation with their own eyes. Each viewer interprets what he sees in terms of his own prejudices. The young are extremely sensitive to injustices of their elders and extremely swift in exercising the judgment errors of their peers. This, unfortunately, cuts both ways.

The school administrator must make every possible attempt to establish a working relationship with the police. *Above all, however, the administrator's primary concern for the safety and welfare of his students and teachers, demands that he recognize the unfortunate polarization which exists between our young and our police and be fully aware of the calculated risk of bringing them into confrontation in highly emotional situations.*

There are times when the police *must* be called if the school administrator is to carry out his obligation for the safety of his students. On the other hand, there are many situations in our tension-ridden schools that can still be handled adequately by school personnel. Some teachers who are otherwise able, cannot or will not become involved in tense group confrontations. Others, however, have the skill, the courage, and the willingness to face these situations and should be utilized before the police are

Maintaining Justice, Law, and Order in the School

called. I have seen excellent preventive work by teachers in near-riot situations, and by no means have they all been the so-called "tough" teachers. Even some women handle this well and are invaluable in controlling the most troublesome and potentially dangerous segment of a potential riot—hysterical female students.

Every school which recognizes the possibility of riots of any kind should have an effective plan to use these people. Such a plan will be outlined below:

Recommendations for Utilizing Police Service

1. Where local police departments have demonstrated excessive brutality and/or strong feelings against youth (this would probably be in small communities with small police forces), every effort should be made to establish emergency liaison with state police.
2. The chief School Administrator should make every effort to establish close and effective relationships with the chief police administrator. Each should contact the other, personally and quickly, on developments of mutual concern.
3. Local police should be used in a variety of resource situations, such as traffic safety and narcotics education. Close and permanent liaison should be established at appropriate levels.
4. When rumors of an impending illegal demonstration or riot develop, the school should contact the police to take advantage of their intelligence reports. Police should be readily available but not too visible. A shift of school personnel should be altered for rapid implementation. Further steps will be outlined below for three basic conditions: *police alerted, police nearby, police take charge.*
5. Efforts should be made to bring non-uniformed police officers into the schools to discuss mutual problems with small groups of students.
6. Efforts should be made to extend special in-service education, such as in human relations, to the police. Beware, however, of confrontation techniques where police will be subjected to abuse, and *above all* test the specific program for effectiveness before inviting the police.
7. Use uniformed police only when absolutely necessary.

THE MAINTENANCE OF LAW AND ORDER

About 40 years ago, a group of young fanatics met in a German beer hall. They were opposed to the Establishment. They wanted immediate reforms. They agitated. They marched the streets. They heckled speakers who disagreed with them. They broke up meetings which espoused "incorrect" viewpoints. The police were unable to (or preferred not to) deal effectively with these young thugs. Law and order broke down. The fanatics seized power and set off a chain of events that led to the murder of millions of people and to the most brutal and costly war in history. How can we, then, treat *law and order* lightly?

We have considered many reasons for the alienation of youth. In later chapters, we will deal with details of *preventive reform*. Let us now consider actions we must take to prevent, contain, and overcome massive physical demonstrations of any sort which may lead to bodily injuries and destruction of property. These may occur suddenly and without warning, but more frequently they are planned either inside or outside the school organization.

Physical demonstrations and disorders take many forms. Each has its unique characteristics which require unique counter-measures. The following guidelines have been developed for *any* type of massive disorder and should be used flexibly of course.

Organization of Personnel for Emergencies

Command: Until and unless the situation becomes so serious that another agency such as the police takes over, *one* school administrator should take complete command. Ordinarily, this should be the chief school administrator. If, for a good reason this power is delegated, the person holding it should not be overruled or interfered with by *anyone* during the period of emergency.

The command person should be at the building where the action is taking place. He should be close to telephones or other communication devices and he should have a portable tape recorder on his person to record instantly all data he deems necessary. If he must be outdoors, he should have a messenger with him to relay required communications quickly.

Liaison: A responsible administrator should be stationed at the central office which can be the information center. He will handle calls to building administrators and to the person in command.

A press liaison administrator should be at the information center. He will make statements to press and radio, carefully recording within the context of each statement the precise time and place it is being released. Recorded radio statements may be repeated over and over throughout the day. Later events may prove them false and most listeners will conclude that they are, thus, on-the-spot lies.

Public information telephones can be manned by secretarial personnel, but they must be close to the information center, *and they must be kept up to date.* When dangerous and false rumors come to them, they will relay these to the press liaison person who will immediately call the local radio station requesting an airing of the true situation.

Security: School personnel at *any* level and from *any* school who can work effectively in emergencies of this type should have been identified in advance. They must be volunteers who will be assigned to an emergency station in the building in question. If two or more buildings are involved, they will be deployed accordingly. They can be relieved of their regular assignments in the usual ways: specialists and non-teaching personnel need no relief. Classroom teachers can exchange assignments with teachers in critical schools who are unable or unwilling to handle massive disorder. Substitutes can be called, for example.

In general these teachers and non-professionals will provide strong supportive coverage, especially in corridors, cafeterias, and other common areas where trouble can appear. Non-professionals can be assigned in pairs to all exits; particularly effective teachers can patrol the grounds if the action is expected inside. If the problem exists outside, another assignment plan must be used depending upon local conditions.

Several teachers with appropriate skills should be assigned as photographers to record events. Each of these should have another physically qualified person with him to prevent a personal attack. Taking photographs of students in a demonstration can be a powerful deterrent to illegal behavior.

Medical: Qualified first aid personnel should be available, on call, by the school nurse. A station wagon may become an improvised ambulance, although the nearest hospital should have been alerted as early as possible. If possible, the school physician should be on hand.

Levels of Preparedness
Normal Condition

Schools which anticipate the remotest possibility of large-scale demonstrations or confrontations (and that could include *all* American secondary schools), should take certain specific precautions *before* trouble starts. Here are some suggestions:

Student identification cards, which include photographs of students holding them, should be used by every middle school or secondary school with an enrollment of over 500 students and, most especially, those over 2,000. *Retention of the cards on the person must be motivated by several clear advantages which the students fully understand.* Yes, regulations should require them and some irritating punishment (paying for a new one, etc.) could be used to enforce them, but the carrot here is more potent than the stick. Discounts of a substantial nature could accrue to the holder at school events, in the school store, etc. It is an easy matter in most places to make the same arrangements at local movie theatres, bowling alleys, and other enterprises.

It is to the distinct advantage of merchants to grant such a discount. I stress this advantage because students have a strong tendency to lose things they do not really want (glasses, galoshes) and it is quite important that most of them actually carry their cards.

When the cards are made out and sealed in plastic, a duplicate can be made for office referral. This could be extremely useful, especially in discipline matters. It would go a long way toward removing the cloak of anonymity which is an annoying problem in large schools.

Visitor's badges should be required in all large secondary

Maintaining Justice, Law, and Order in the School

schools. These should be of the type used in industry which clip on clothing and are easily identified.

Resource teachers brought in from other buildings in times of tension or trouble should also wear badges of a distinct color for identification purposes. Students and teachers within the building should know who all adult strangers are. Some will consider this an imposition and, perhaps, an overaction. It can save a great deal of trouble when the chips are down.

Emergency guidelines should be printed and available to all teachers. Some procedures must, of course, be kept confidential. These can be relayed by word of mouth. Many procedures will develop out of the nature of the specific problem. It is necessary to brief teachers on the broad nature of these emergency guidelines and to stress the value of common sense and flexibility. It does no harm for students to see these guidelines. It is, on the contrary, a fair and reasonable matter for them to know where the lines are drawn.

Printed handouts describing the legal authority for any possible administrative action should be available.

All teachers should be briefed on the importance of restraint in using force and of having witnesses identified in any crucial situation involving the use of force by anyone.

Alert Condition

All of the precautions described above may be used at any level of emergency. When conflicting or unconfirmed rumors of trouble appear, it would be wise to alert all personnel that they may be involved in a possible crisis, so that they are ready for a sudden call. Police should also be involved, especially in analyzing the validity of the rumors.

Potentially Dangerous Condition

When strong and consistent rumors are confirmed by the police, the following steps would be indicated:

1. Emergency teachers and other personnel are called to duty. A heavy coverage should be provided for bus unloading and all areas where large groups can gather. Corridors are especially dangerous.

2. Police should be alerted and available, but uniformed police or marked police cars should not be in prominent display.
3. Gang leaders should be picked up and either isolated under supervision or driven home for temporary suspension for their own safety and for the safety of others. Names of people on such suspension should be made available to teachers periodically through *internal* communications.
4. Security and communications precautions outlined above should be enforced. Pay stations should be deactivated by arrangement with the telephone company to prevent wild rumors from spreading or enforcements being called for by gangs.
5. Administrators and/or guidance offices must be secured, drawers locked, and papers removed.
6. The campus is closed to outsiders. Outside patrols should have walkie-talkie radios. Visitors will be carefully screened at the doors by teachers and administrators.

Dangerous Condition

When violence erupts, every effort must be made to contain it immediately. As soon as it becomes apparent that it cannot be contained by school personnel, two things must happen immediately:

1. The police are given complete control and command and all personnel are to cooperate with them completely.
2. Buses must be made available (they should be standing by) under heavy supervision, and the school will be closed until it can reopen with reasonable assurance of the safety of its students.

We are living in difficult and dangerous times. We must have courage and the determination to protect the safety and welfare of school personnel and students by firm and decisive action when it becomes necessary.

7

> ... any program to educate or train people outside or apart from the mainstream where the majority are educated will be seen as second class by those enrolled, by those who employ the trainees, and by those who must pay the bill, the taxpayers.
>
> Grant Venn [1]

Working with Alienated Youth

Various abnormalities and exceptionalities among students in our schools have received greatly increased attention in recent years and have even stimulated a significant increase in financial support at all levels. Like all our educational efforts, however, the support is uneven, with the poorest services going to the poorest schools, which need them most. Through special classes within districts and various types of jointures; county, state, and federal programs; and tuition payments to specialized private schools, we have attempted to

---

[1] Grant Venn, *Man, Education, and Manpower,* (Washington, D.C., American Association of School Administrators, 1970), p. 7.

remediate the special problems of the retarded, the gifted, the emotionally disturbed, and the physically handicapped among our students. This chapter will deal with a type of exceptionality which causes our greatest discipline problems, upon which we have utilized our least creative efforts, and with which we have had the least success. Simply stated, this is the problem of the student who has normal or better ability, cannot benefit from other exceptional programs, and is so alienated from school programs that he has turned off his learning process.

Along with our usual practice of providing the best for the wealthiest districts, we have also concentrated our efforts in exceptional education toward the youngest students, with consequent neglect at the higher levels. It is not uncommon, for example, to provide special programs for emotionally disturbed students up to the age of 11 or 12 and cut off the services completely at that point. This adds substantially to the already formidable problems of the intermediate upper school, whether it is called a middle school or a junior high school. Thus, we find the dramatic storm center of American education in our urban junior high schools. These schools serve enormous numbers of alienated young adolescents who hate school and are imprisoned there by well-intended laws that only permit them to leave if they are better served by another type of institution (if there is room for them). Urban junior high schools generally operate in an atmosphere of perpetual frustration. Worse yet, it is now generally known that relatively little effective teaching occurs in the most troubled of these schools.

From the viewpoint of school discipline, the most neglected exceptional child in our public schools is the alienated young adolescent who despises school but must remain there. He is not emotionally disturbed to the degree required for admission to that type of institution. He has not been convicted of breaking enough laws to be admitted to that type of institution. He is too young to leave school legally as a dropout. (In some states, this age is as high as 18!) So he remains in the school he hates, interfering with the education of others and driving his teachers and administrators wild. And his name is legion.

The logic of the law seems to be that the schools have, at least, contributed to his state of alienation and it is up to them to deal with the problem. The courts, recognizing the inadequacies of the home and the school in many cases, also recognize the often greater inadequacies of mental and "correctional" institutions. Thus, they repeatedly utilize probation as the lesser of several evils and return the young offender to school.

The schools want desperately to solve this problem of exceptionality but too often have simply provided more of the same—more carrot or more stick. The "get tough" approach so beloved in simplistic thought has been worse than useless in dealing with alienated adolescents. It simply compounds the problem. Permissiveness, by itself, creates only cynical contempt on the part of the alienated students and deep resentment on the part of students who play the game according to the rules.

The greatest hurdle in solving this knotty problem is, perhaps, the formidable defense mechanism of American schools. Long accustomed to being blamed for all the ills of our society, school people are loath to admit any flaws within the schools. They point, with some logic, to solutions *outside* the school, costly solutions such as more meaningful guidance for inadequate parents, more enlightened and better supported correctional institutions, etc. This is a fine dream, but we must face reality. It is a fact that apart from our military establishment and our space enterprises, our public schools in recent years have been blessed with the greatest increase of tax support of all our institutions. It hardly seems logical that in the foreseeable future our mental and correctional institutions will benefit from higher tax priorities than our schools. If we concede that the schools have contributed to the problem, that the schools suffer most from the problem, and that the schools are receiving comparatively better support than other institutions, does it not follow that the schools must make a much greater effort to alleviate the problem and stop blaming other institutions?

GETTING STARTED

Educational problem solving usually starts with a committee. Solutions to educational problems usually contain the same elements: (1) hire more personnel; (2) select the best teachers; (3) give them small classes and substantial supportive assistance; (4) give them the best possible spaces and equipment; (5) spend more money.

Anticipating that this process will be duplicated and that these recommendations will be made, perhaps we can list some facts which must be faced if any progress is to be made:

1. A school district which can identify a significant number of young adolescents who are alienated from learning must be doing *something* wrong. Schools cannot accept all of the blame nor can they accept none of the blame.
2. The major goal must not simply be remediation but a correction of the conditions which led to alienation in the first place.
3. Something substantially different in the way of learning experiences must be provided to turn on the alienated youngsters again.
4. Most alienated students need what all students need—good teaching. They are like normal students, only more so.
5. There are some interesting and successful programs to study. Everyone does not have to start from point zero.

TO SEGREGATE OR NOT TO SEGREGATE

The Segregation of Exceptional Students

In the citation at the beginning of this chapter, Venn points out one of the well-known evils of segregation within our schools. Others are painfully apparent: the superiority complex of the students in a gifted class; the inferiority complex of the students in a slow class; the poignant wistfulness of the crippled child in a special group.

There are, of course, compelling reasons for some types of segregation: the special physical needs of crippled youngsters; the special education needs of the blind and the deaf children; etc. Since we are dealing here with a type of exceptionality that often robs other children of their opportunities to learn, we must deal with the question of segregation in a pragmatic way. *There are times when segregation is absolutely essential.* It should be utilized only when it *is* essential, and the goal of any program for exceptional children should be integration.

Perhaps the best example of the wise utilization of segregation and integration in education would be the story of a student I was privileged to know a few years ago. Totally blind and crippled by polio, this girl received her special education (Braille, etc.) in a segregated school. When she was ready for secondary school, she attended alternately the special and a regular school. Later she attended a regular high school with only the minimal support of special recorded and Braille materials and graduated with her non-handicapped classmates.

Many techniques have been used with little success in dealing with the problem of alienated early adolescents who disturb classes and fail to respond to the usual doses of discipline and/or guidance. In some cities, they are transferred from one school to another. During their initial insecurity period in their new surroundings, their aggressiveness is temporarily subdued. Usually this lasts until they have established new peer relationships with other anti-social youths in their new school. Now and then a borderline case will truly "turn over a new leaf" when given this opportunity, but the basic conditions are probably about the same and sooner or later the alienated youngster rejects the new situation for the same reasons he rejected the old one.

Too often these youngsters are merely taken out of their classes and forced to sit somewhere, under supervision, for a day or even a week. Long accustomed to boredom, they seem to serve their terms as exiles peacefully. Some even seem to enjoy it, especially if they are seated in an office where people are coming and going and things are happening. This, I suppose, would be an appropriate type of training for professional flagpole sitters.

Occasionally one of these students becomes fortunate enough to have a dedicated and stubborn teacher take a sustained interest in him and demonstrate that someone really cares. When this happens, one of the minor miracles of education may occur. The problem here is that this teacher must now devote an inordinate amount of time and effort to one student, possibly to the detriment of his other 100 to 150 charges. It is remarkable, perhaps, that so many teachers find real satisfaction in this type of intensive care. They are the people to turn to when the school is ready to move toward a realistic solution of the problem.

Like our hospitals, every school faced with the problem of alienated students who do not fit into the existing exceptional program needs an *Intensive Care Unit* to rehabilitate these academic drifters, many of whom have normal or superior verbal potential.

The question of segregation answers itself. When an alienated youngster interferes with the learning opportunities, safety, health, or well-being of the other students, *he must be segregated from them.* He must remain segregated until he is ready to return. This can be done gradually and partially, and it should be done with appropriate support and a close liaison between the teacher of the segregated class and the teacher in the regular receiving class.

There are at least three legitimate reasons for the segregation of alienated youngsters for a reasonable period of time:

1. The danger to others is mentioned above. It can also be argued that a separation from school of a repeated offender has a salutary effect on other students. It also dramatizes to the offender that his problem is being considered at a new level of seriousness. To put it bluntly, he has broken the rules and something has happened to him.
2. The need to create a positive attitude toward learning, "to turn the student on" again.
3. The need to experiment with new methods and materials in a model setting and stimulate their use throughout the school district.

The goal must, of course, be the earliest possible return of the student to the mainstream of education so that others may benefit from what is certain to be relatively expensive Intensive Care Units. Let us examine three sample programs, each of which illustrates a different approach to segregation of alienated students:

A SEPARATE SCHOOL

The Philadelphia Advancement School

Originated in North Carolina under the sponsorship of *The Learning Institute of North Carolina* and operated for three years as a laboratory school for research into the problems of dealing with underachievers, the school ran into problems in March of 1968 with the State Department of Public Instruction over autonomy of operation.

In searching for a new location, the director was approached by Mark R. Shedd, the unorthodox and creative new superintendent of the Philadelphia Public Schools. Accepting a calculated risk that a program that worked in the rural South would also work in a large city, the director, Peter Brittenweiser and a portion of his staff moved into an abandoned industrial warehouse in Philadelphia which was purchased by the school district to house the school.

Here, indeed, was something different, very different from any school in the city. Designed to serve able but alienated students who were consistent academic failures by the time they reached the seventh grade, the school underwent an initial period of shock as the teachers faced a new breed of city kids who were tougher, more cynical, and much more aggressive than their former students in North Carolina.

The approaches to learning employed in this unusual school are thought by some to resemble the best of what was developed in the progressive schools in the thirties. Students are involved in planning their learning experience. They do things physically. "Learning in the marrow bone" becomes as important as learning in the brain. The ancient fetish about extrinsic motivation is taken with a grain of salt as very tangible and immediate rewards follow successful learning. A game called "stud spelling" combines the excitement of poker (which the kids love) with the drudgery of learning to spell (which they hate). Play money is sometimes supplemented with even more meaningful prizes. Teachers visit each other's classes to learn from each other. This is considered heresy in most conventional schools. Teachers assume responsibility for the behavior of *all* the students, not just "their own."

The communications program leans heavily on creative expression and is based on the notion that ideas come first and the mechanics of English will follow. This poses a problem, of course, when a student returns to a conventional classroom, where he will be downgraded for his grammar and spelling, illustrating the great need for follow-up when the students have finished their one-semester experience in the Philadelphia Advancement School.

Although the degree of permissiveness and freedom of expression in the school may initially shock the visitor, he quickly learns that there are rules of behavior—very familiar ones.

Students and teachers meet in "family groups," generally composed of teachers and the students they meet daily in class. One of the goals of this grouping is to assist students with their problems in relating to teachers and other students. Each student signs a "contract" when he enters the school, stating what is expected of the school and what is expected of him. Sample agreements: "No smoking; no fighting; no stealing or destruction of property; no abusive language or behavior; no wandering through the building."

In addition to the contract, the family groups draw up "secondary regulations" which also sound familiar. They are concerned with off-limits spaces, running, throwing objects, cafeteria behavior, etc. Thus, a student learns that his freedom and rights are restricted by the freedom and rights of his peers. Next to an improvement in his attitude about learning, this is probably the most important factor in a successful return to the conventional classroom.

Here, then, is a model of a school that segregates able but alienated city youngsters and then returns them to their old environment, hopefully "turned on" to learning and better prepared to relate effectively to their teachers and their peers. More significantly, perhaps, is the school's goal of providing better materials and methods through experimentation so that all the city's classrooms will "turn on" kids to learning. We can only hope that it is not a case of too little too late. In the summer of 1970, the Philadelphia School District faced the possibility of not being able to open in September because of a lack of funds and a possible teacher's strike. One prominent black leader in Philadelphia commented that these schools should remain closed for 20 years, "They aren't teaching ghetto kids anything anyhow." Regardless of the merits of this observation, it is a frightening thing to hear.

A SCHOOL WITHIN A SCHOOL

The Chicago Ray School

An even smaller drop of excellence in an even larger pond is the *Independent Learning Center* at the Ray School in Chicago. Located near the University of Chicago, this school draws students from two different worlds, the world of the university and the world of the black ghetto.

Students are assigned to the one-room center on teacher recommendation for varying periods of time. There they encounter a federally funded cornucopia of learning materials, teachers, and special consultants at a ratio of six to one. They are encouraged to pursue learning experiences which interest them and to do so independently with frequent encouragement but with no evaluative grades.

Students are given all sorts of options and are provided an opportunity to succeed in an environment *that differs from their regular classroom experience.* Follow-up is relatively easy since all the students are enrolled in the same school. Approximately 200 of the Ray School's 900 students use the center regularly, and communications between the Learning Center Staff and the other teachers can be easily managed.

A pattern similar to the Philadelphia Advancement School has developed. Freedom of expression, observing the rights of others, and experience-related learning appear to be the order of the day. The flexibility of movement here would seem to be a tremendous advantage. Students can, for example, utilize the center for a short period of time each day. There is no real segregation. Teachers in conventional classes are closer to the materials and methods being used in the Center. One would presume that this would cause a more effective spin-off from the experimental to the conventional classroom. If this plan were to be multiplied throughout Chicago, however, serious problems of cost and efficiency of operation would be involved. Perhaps the solution might be in the creation of several large centers with a satellite station in each school.

A SCHOOL APART AND WITHIN

The Bristol Township Opportunity School

Levittown is a community located in the second ring of suburbs north of Philadelphia and a few minutes south of Trenton, New Jersey. The school district serves 15,000 students of largely lower middle class origins and a relatively small ghetto population. Disciplinary problems, especially drug usage, reflect the proximity of the two cities.

In 1968, a beginning effort was made concerning the problem of dealing with alienated seventh and eighth grade boys. Girls were excluded at first because it was felt that the overt behavior problems of boys were more pressing at that time. Later efforts to include girls have been thwarted by lack of space, money, and appropriate personnel. The program is financed entirely by the district.

A staff was selected, consisting of two male teachers and the contracted part-time support of a psychiatrist and a psychiatric social worker. A Salvation Army building was rented and the process of selecting students was begun. The teachers were selected on the basis of their interest and because they were coaches who related well with boys. It was felt that an opportunity to improve athletic skills would be attractive to these boys. The psychiatrist had an unusual grasp of school problems and public school environment. The building was ideal in many ways, complete with recreational and cooking facilities, including a pool table.

The first problem was the adjustment of the teachers to this type of boy whom they seldom encountered on their football squads. The traditional arsenal of the football coach had to be exchanged for new and more subtle weaponry. Adjustment was painful at times but the assistance of the psychiatrist was priceless. Good things began to happen.

One of the more valuable (and sometimes amusing) devices used was a daily journal describing the problems encountered and the actions taken. This journal provided invaluable assistance in adjusting the program for its second year of operation. Having studied the Philadelphia Advancement School closely, much was borrowed from the experiences of that institution. Although the Bristol Township students were selected largely on the basis of alienation rather than underachievement, there was much to be learned from the Philadelphia experiment.

Major changes took place in the second and third years. The students were not segregated, for example, for the entire day. They spent a half day at the Opportunity School and a half day in their regular school. This eliminated some of the academic problems of having teachers attempt to cover all subjects. Bringing in resource teachers did not work out in practice as it had appeared in planning. A much greater emphasis was placed on supportive service in the regular classroom and in working with parents (often through home visits during the day).

Although the maximum number of boys involved at one time has been about 15, and although many problems have been encountered, there is a strong feeling on the part of the staff involved that the program should be continued and expanded. Far more traditional in approach than the Chicago or the Philadelphia programs, it is now felt that the teachers involved would benefit significantly from an exchange program with the nearby Philadelphia Advancement School. Perhaps this could be a third goal for such a program—the improvement of education for alienated youth in other districts.

General Recommendations for Non-Segregated Treatment

1. Before any progress can be made, the school district must face squarely the nature and extent of the problem. It must identify and acknowledge *its* part in creating the problem and directly attack the conditions which caused it. This seems like a very simple move, but for some reason it is not.
2. The district must face the question of whether or not it has enough severely alienated students to provide a segregated learning center for them.
3. The segregated learning center must be staffed by sensitive but realistic teachers who have been given adequate in-service education by people who truly understand the problem. They must learn to select and develop new methods, rules, and materials to accommodate the learning styles of alienated youngsters.

4. Re-entry into conventional classes must be provided for by part-time segregation and strong supportive services in the home and in the school. It is particularly important to have regular conferences with the teachers of these students in the home school. A trained social worker should be involved.
5. Every effort should be made to avoid grouping badly alienated students together in slow classes, especially in subjects such as art and industrial arts where a great deal of self-discipline must be invoked. In far too many schools, these youngsters are placed in classes with slow learners whether or not they are able to handle more difficult work. Thus they travel through the school together, driving teachers wild and absolutely ruining the education of slower learners who may have good attitudes toward school. An alienated student with normal ability and poor achievement is far better off in a normal academic class than he is with a group of other alienated youngsters and slow learners.
6. Regardless of how these young people are grouped, they must be challenged up to the level of their ability. Too often they blackmail teachers into not assigning demanding learning tasks. This is inexcusable.
7. A combination of understanding, mutual respect, fair but firm treatment, and a strict adherence to the rules of good teaching is the only sensible prescription for this school problem. Sometimes a brief, friendly chat with a teacher on some subject, *other than the student's problems,* can do a great deal of good. I am painfully aware that there are times when all of the components of this prescription fail. *That* is the time to start thinking about a segregated setting outside of the school.

It is clear that a major effort must be made in this neglected area of exceptionality—the alienated early adolescent who has been turned off by conventional teaching. It may not stand up under close scrutiny as a discrete research entity since it overlaps other allied efforts in the education of the emotionally disturbed and the disadvantaged. It also overlaps the entire mainstream of public education. It is here, perhaps, that we can justify great increases in time, effort, and money. If we learn to turn on alienated youngsters, we may learn how to stop turning off *any* youngsters to the joy of learning.

8

> The devilish seductivity of human relations training stems from the fact that it can reduce individual resistance to change more effectively than any other known means. It promises the wishful decision maker, therefore, that his desires for school reform can be fulfilled.
>
> Max Birnbaum [1]

Human Relations Education

Human relations training began, I suppose, when man started to communicate with man with something more sophisticated than a club. Evidence of its utilization can be found in ancient civilizations. More recently it can be noted that the Quakers have used group dynamics in their meetings for over 300 years. What is new, however, is the application of this artistic science or scientific art to industrial organizations and, even more recently, to the implementation of change in education and the teaching process itself.

For those who value these things, a point in time which

---

[1] Max Birnbaum, "Sense About Sensitivity Training," *Saturday Review*, November 15, 1969, p. 97.

may be recorded as the beginning of a renaissance in human relations training in America is 1947. In that year, the National Training Laboratory was founded in Bethel, Maine. Several pioneers made major contributions and overcame formidable obstacles in the refinement of the process but it seems fair to single out one as the father of modern human relations training, Leland Bradford of the National Training Laboratory.[2]

TYPES OF HUMAN RELATIONS TRAINING

There are probably as many approaches to human relations training as there are trainers. It is not unusual for gifted students of great trainers to deviate from the style of the masters when they are working alone. There are, however, certain basic patterns which remain relatively uniform.

The core of human relations training (or sensitivity training as some prefer to call it) is Carl Rogers' "T group" or training group of 10 to 15 people who meet in an unstructured and unthreatening atmosphere, for extended periods of time, under the guidance of a trainer who has the skills and experience necessary to *optimize the learning process*.

T groups meet for lengthy daily sessions (12 hours or more is not uncommon) for periods ranging from two days to two weeks. The longer sessions are called marathons. The participant is assisted in examining the how and why of group formation, the manner in which individuals assume various roles, and the way his role emerges. It must be emphasized that *"T" means training, not therapy*. Because of recent attention in the mass media to group therapy as applied to the emotionally disturbed, the criminal recidivist, and the drug addict, there is a tendency for many to assume that human relations training uses the same approach. An emotionally disturbed person does not belong in a T group. He will probably suffer harm and he may destroy the experience for others.

The type of training used must be determined by the *purpose* of the training. In school applications it would, in my opin-

---

[2] Ibid.

ion, be wise to ignore the more controversial and avant-garde approaches and concentrate on two *goals* which are not necessarily mutually exclusive. The question is where do you want your major thrust, on individual growth or on the solution of specific group problems? A decision for emphasis must be made because it will determine the nature of the entire program. In recent years, most school districts have turned to a concerted human relations training program in desperation. All the usual processes have failed. It therefore seems logical to set a goal of solving or decreasing the problems which led to the despair. Individual growth should become an ancillary goal, but one which is an inseparable part of the major goal. When teachers discover that racial tension, for example, decreases significantly as their behavior changes, they will be strongly motivated to change their behavior.

Thus we oversimplify types of training for school use in terms of two major purposes: (1) problem solving, (2) individual improvement. In the latter portion of this chapter, I will describe a major human relations program which was directed toward a major goal of problem solving and draw from the evaluation data which should be helpful to a school district planning a similar program.

BY-PRODUCTS OF HUMAN RELATIONS TRAINING

The preceding intentional overemphasis on major goals calls for further clarification of lesser (but important) goals. When a school district is paralyzed by racial violence, it can see but one major goal. First there must be peace. Then there must be significant changes in the conditions which created the violence. *Some,* but not all of these conditions, can be improved by teachers, administrators, and school board members. Some, which are not controlled by the school, can be improved with the assistance of the school through an extension of its human relations program into the community. Specific examples of this will appear later in the chapter. It has become obvious to many of us in education that the reconstructionists of four decades ago were right in insisting that schools must change society, not isolate themselves from it. I am convinced that we have been too fearful of facing this challenge openly for too long. Perhaps even now it is too late.

In examining the significant by-products of human relations training, we quickly see the important function of effecting necessary but difficult curriculum change. One prime example of this is in the area of subgroup identity.

The melting pot purpose of American public schools has failed so badly that not too many more words should be wasted on it. Our public schools have failed to unify our nation and they have failed as an active agent of upward mobility for the lower classes. At best they have extended mediocrity throughout our land. In spite of the strength of plurality in American society, however, the basically unified school curriculum lingers on. Slowly and painfully, and in response to enormous militancy, a patchwork of change has been added to the old structure. Feeble scholastically and bedeviled by instant expertise, it has to date only purchased time. In 1969, for example, Mexican-Americans in Los Angeles asserted themselves through violence in search of identity for their group.

This is an example of an important area of curriculum change in which human relations education can serve several purposes. It can increase awareness among teachers as to the need for changes in methods and materials to accommodate the learning styles of various minority groups. It can accelerate acceptance of these groups as legitimate and unique entities in American society. And it can make teachers more receptive to change from a melting pot curriculum to a curriculum of and for diversity.

Let us list a few legitimate reasons why *any* school district (with or without a current crisis) should explore the idea of implementing a thorough program of human relations training:

1. To counter all types of prejudice with accurate information.
2. To present to all possible minority groups viable and continuous alternatives to violence as a method of protest.
3. To better equip teachers to work with increasingly hostile and militant students and subgroups.
4. To improve attitudes of everyone toward everyone else.

Human Relations Education

5. To effect desirable change.
6. To help teachers to understand the role of emotions in teaching and learning.

PITFALLS TO AVOID

Opposition to human relations training is still formidable and it is not without validity. It comes from many and varied sources and for a host of different reasons. The administrator who is planning a program should be prepared to face criticism and skepticism and can be armed in advance if he takes a few precautionary steps. The major critical thrusts will probably come in five major patterns:

1. This program is a waste of money and time. Teachers are taken out of the classroom and the children are left to substitutes. This criticism cannot be dismissed lightly. A good program *is* expensive, especially if many substitutes are hired to release teachers. Curiously, much of this will come from teachers *before they have partaken of the human relations experience or early in the process.* For the most part, it is a manifestation of fear. When it is clearly established that the experience should *improve* instruction and make it easier for the teacher, this criticism will diminish. It is the responsibility of the trainer to teach for transfer; then we will not face the damning question from a teacher *after the program is completed,* "O.K. I'm all sensitized. I love everybody. Now what do I *do* tomorrow when I face my 30 kids?"

2. The resistance of a bigot to "brainwashing" is another serious matter. No teacher should be forced to undergo training. No hard-core bigot should be invited to the experience. At best it will be a painful waste of time. Very few bona fide miracles occur in training groups.

3. The extreme right wing automatically rejects human relations training as brainwashing from the left. The simple truth is that effective human relations training is the exact opposite of brainwashing. The person who has been subjected to years of bigoted brainwashing in his home has an opportunity to cleanse himself and begin to develop objective attitudes. The problem here is that ineptly handled training, especially if

it involves encounter techniques, may serve to *strengthen* bigotry!

4. The allegation that this training includes therapy and amateur psychiatry is not entirely false. Again, the way to minimize this charge is to utilize qualified trainers who know their limits and avoid including any emotionally unbalanced person in the process. Trainees as well as trainers should be carefully selected.

5. The most penetrating criticism of human relations training is that widespread charlatanism has accompanied its rapid growth. Instant experts have a tendency to cluster around any new movement in education. Human relations training is especially attractive to these patent medicine drummers in education because no substantial accreditation or licensure has yet been created to protect us. In his superb article cited earlier in this chapter, Max Birnbaum points out that,

> Two kinds of sensitivity training are particularly susceptible today to exploitation by the enthusiastic amateur or the enterprising entrepreneur: the area of non-verbal experience and the confrontation session. Each requires a minimum of experience and knowledge to stimulate an initial response . . . but in each case a maximum of expert knowledge and sophistication is required to extract a positive educational outcome. The most damning judgment that can be made about the non-verbal field is that a small bag of easily learned exercises, plus several 33⅓ rpm records, makes anyone a trainer . . .

Avoiding Mistakes

All five areas of criticism above can be avoided or minimized by careful planning *and by selecting the right trainer*. There are several ways to exercise caution:

1. Heed the ancient Packard automobile slogan, "Ask the man who owns one." In a school district, the chief administrator should first call his opposite number in a district which has been seriously involved in human relations training. If the initial response is positive, a request should be made for a meeting between the personnel about to be deeply involved and the people who have been involved.

2. The chief administrator and the person about to be most heavily involved should attend a training workshop.

3. Write for information to: (a) The Boston University Human Relations Laboratory, 120 East 56th Street, New York, N.Y. 10022, or (b) The National Training Laboratories Institute, 1201 16th St. NW, Washington, D.C. 20036.
4. If you have serious doubts about the program and if you cannot obtain the services of a completely reliable trainer, postpone action. This is one program that cannot result merely in wasted time and money if it fails. Serious harm can be done.
5. Before embarking on a program, consult with your trainer about the width and depth of it. Too limited a program, even if successful, can be a waste of time. Your object should be to influence behavior in as many classrooms as possible.
6. Check out possible federal funding and foundation funding. Use the *Foundation Directory* published by the Russell Sage Foundation, 230 Park Avenue, New York City.

CASE HISTORY OF A TRAINING PROGRAM

Bristol Township, Pennsylvania is a residential community in suburban Philadelphia consisting mostly of the least expensive Levitt houses constructed in response to job opportunities created in the early fifties by the building of a major industrial plant in the area. In a real sense it was an "instant community," very rapidly built in what had been a rural section of Bucks County.

Many of the 70,000 inhabitants came from coal regions where jobs were scarce. Others came from Philadelphia to seek a better life in suburbia. About 8% were Negroes. Almost all of the rest were whites. Many of the blacks, including the most economically disadvantaged, lived in an apartment complex of barracks-like design which had been constructed to meet housing needs for industrial workers during World War II. Efforts of black citizens to purchase houses in the white community were sharply resisted early in the history of the township. Today there is still very little housing integration.

In 1967 the black students from the barracks complex were distributed among other schools in the district in an effort to desegregate the schools closest to the apartments. This move took courage and resolution on the part of the school board and, initially, surprisingly little opposition was voiced in the community.

The usual resentment about bussing for desegregation persisted however. For many of the citizens (those from the coal regions), this was their first real experience with integration. Extremely few Negroes live in the coal areas of Pennsylvania. For the people who had fled from Philadelphia, this represented a threat. Some of them felt that they had made great sacrifices in escaping to suburbia. Now the problems of the city were catching up with them again. To compound the problem, many of the black children were very unhappy with being bussed to strange schools in which they were a very small and very visible minority.

Like the citizenry, many of the teachers in Bristol Township came from the coal country where they had had no experience in teaching black children. Many others came from Philadelphia and some had had negative experiences in black-white relationships.

The same problems existed in the police force and among political leaders. The need for a massive human relations training program became very clear when serious racial incidents occurred in the secondary schools. Research, as indicated previously, led to the Boston University School of Human Relations center in Manhattan and Professor Max Birnbaum. A proposal was prepared under the provisions of Title IV, Section 405 of Public Law 88-352, The "Civil Rights Act" of 1964. It was approved for $157,353 for a program to run for 15 months and an evaluation to be conducted about a year after the conclusion of the training program.

The objective of the program was to train all professional staff members in the skills and techniques of human relations and minority problems in order to reduce tensions and alleviate problems arising from majority-minority relationships. It was further projected to train members of the community, including police, for the same purposes in order to insure a cooperative school-community approach to the solution of the problems. The ideal objective was the achievement of a climate of mutual acceptance and respect for all people and a reflection of this in the curriculum and the ethos of the schools in the community.

The training was conducted outside the schools in a nearby motel in order to avoid the usual interruptions and distractions.

It was divided into two phases: (1) week-long leadership training sessions designed to produce skilled leaders able to work primarily with adults in the reduction of tensions and alleviation of problems; (2) two-day workshop sessions designed to produce staff and community personnel skilled in human relations and majority-minority problems and able to work primarily with students.

Three week-long sessions were held, each attended by 25 professional staff members and two or three community representatives. Twenty-five two-day sessions, each attended by 32 people chosen from the staff and the community, were spaced over the 15 months. All sessions were conducted to surface personal feelings as an initial step in recognition, and progressed to a development of sensitivity to the needs and problems of others, especially members of minority groups, and to the development of skill techniques for handling problems and reducing tensions.

An important part of the program was the development of a cadre of trained teachers who would continue the work with adults after the formal program was completed. These 75 people represented 10% of the total staff, and all of them attended the week-long sessions. Two were from the central office and were selected because of their specific responsibilities in the areas of intergroup education and personnel work. The remaining 73 were chosen proportionately from all 15 buildings on the basis of their influence with their peers, except that in the secondary schools one had to be an administrator and one a counselor.

The program proceeded on schedule, with only minimal and predictable difficulties. Although it was difficult for participants to assess the overall value of the program, a number of extremely visible and dramatic signs seemed to indicate that, at least, the program had created no damage. Avenues of communication had been institutionalized for adults and students in the form of intergroup councils. Racial incidents were substantially reduced and those that did take place involved few students. A perceptible improvement in school spirit was established in the schools which had been storm centers. Students were communicating with each other and with adults.

An outside evaluation was essential, however, in order to obtain perspective and clear vision. This was undertaken by Dr. Gregory M. O'Brien and Dr. Morton H. Elfenbein. The result was a lengthy and scholarly report substantially intended to improve the process through intelligent case study. For our purposes here, I shall excerpt material that would be useful to educators who are about to become involved in or who have been involved in the implementation of a human relations program *from the school end of the venture.*

In Bristol Township, the decisions for change and for utilizing human relations training in that change originated in the central administration, was approved by the board, and was generally supported by the principals. Thus among the first people to undergo training were these very people.

Support from above can prevent sabotage but, by itself, it cannot insure success in a program of change. In recognition of this, cadres of teachers chosen for their peer influence qualities received early training in the program.

Survey instruments and interviews were used to determine the following behavioral indexes of change:

- Personal openness to change.
- Attitudes toward student behavior.
- Problem awareness (in intergroup relations).
- Attitudes toward discipline.
- Isolation or alienation from administration.
- Perceived limits of teacher's role.
- Attitudes toward human relations program and cadre.
- Linkages between school and community and parents.

Results were, as anticipated, mixed, but it is significant to note that participants in the program were not generally reluctant to talk frankly about it, whether their reactions were positive, negative, or mixed. As a personal observation, it became clear to me that in some cases (which came to my attention by accident) teachers who had been reserved and quiet had "opened up" after their training experience and would talk freely and frankly, at least about human relations.

The evaluation focused attention on an important point in its analysis of the process of selecting teachers for the cadre. In

Human Relations Education

the case studied, the principals had selected the teachers and had had, in truth, very little useful briefing before the act. O'Brien and Elfenbein suggested that the following criteria might have been used. I agree completely and paraphrase these criteria for the benefit of educators who are planning a similar training program:

1. The individual should express interest—or at least willingness to participate in the additional training and work during the year. This intent should be assessed prior to selection of personnel for training.
2. The individuals selected should be acceptable to both faculty and principals since they will have to work closely with each group. One way would be to have the principal pick the cadre from a group of people selected by the faculty.
3. It seems that cadre members who have been faculty leaders in other activities have been more successful in providing leadership in the intergroup area. This is not always the case, particularly among minority group members, whose experiences have prepared them to be of particular help in discussions of intergroup problems. This can be a first time for some individuals to have an opportunity for leadership, but the potential must be there. Real leadership ability is needed for cadre membership in a successful human relations program.

A number of the conclusions reached by the evaluation team would seem to be applicable to any school district. I have paraphrased such recommendations by O'Brien and Elfenbein:

1. A continuation of the commitment by those in authority is a necessary condition for a successful change effort. Unless the institution of a human relations program is perceived by the members of an organizational system as a *permanent* (a very long term) commitment of the system, the effectiveness of the program will be minimal. A program perceived as temporary, as a strategy for cooling off a tense situation, cannot effect any real change. (*Note:* In the district studies, Bristol Township, Pa., a permanent, full-time position was created for a coordinator of human relations. The person selected has been working within the schools and in the community to perpetuate the machinery of intergroup communications created after the first crisis.)

2. One of the major factors accounting for the success experienced in the Bristol Township program is the identification and utilization of particular individuals whose capabilities in the area of intergroup relations are exceptional. In other words, seek out talent at home and *use* it. It goes without saying that the best way to use a talented person is to give him reasonable time to do what you want to do and support him while he is doing it. Continually adding tasks to the duties of exceptional teachers is neither fair nor efficient.

3. In schools where power was more widely shared in the change effort, there seemed to be a more effective program and a climate of greater openness to change on the part of students, faculty, and parents. As we interpret this, *if power remains centralized and access to the centralized power is denied to persons with designated-change agent roles (cadre) or roles as participants in the change process (intergroup councils and concerned faculty), change will be less likely to occur.*

4. Starting training with central authorities and others of major responsibility and power is quite functional for increasing the openness to change within an educational system.

5. The strategy of establishing a cadre group within each school is a sound one. By identification and training of not just one but a group of individuals in each school, an intra-organizational group to support the individual cadre members in their efforts to expedite changes is provided. Having more than one *active* cadre member in each school seems essential for any meaningful change.

POSTSCRIPT

If the Bristol Township human relations program were to be evaluated solely and simplistically in terms of improved black-white relationships, it must on the surface be given a failing grade. Racial problems appeared again in the year following the end of the formal training sessions. In the spring of 1971, the upper (grades 11 and 12) high school became a storm center of racial clashes. The following excerpts are taken from a first-page story by Mike Renshaw which appeared in the March 31, 1971 edition of the *Bucks County Courier Times*.

Attendance dips sharply
Police Patrolling Wilson Corridors

Classes resumed this morning at Woodrow Wilson High School under the watchful eye of 12 Bristol Township policemen.

Wearing riot helmets, police lined the corridors. Two police dogs were also inside the school. There were no incidents when students arrived for classes.

• • • • • •

These actions grew out of yesterday's melee in which two teachers and seven students were injured.

Let us look beneath the surface and consider some facts which must be considered in evaluating this program or any program of human relations training.

1. No program of any type can turn back the tide of a nation-wide revolt which is led by extremists and opposed, in part, by extremists. A small group of fanatics can cause violence anywhere at any time if they are determined to do so. No human relations program has, to my knowledge, claimed that it would solve this problem. No program can prevent the clash of determined extremists. No program can change the thinking of a determined fanatic.

2. A good human relations program can, at best, *buy time*. It did buy time in Bristol Township during which significant changes were made. Even these changes could not deter the battle plans of dedicated extremists, but having been present in these schools during these years, I am convinced that conditions would have been much worse without the training program.

3. The human relations program seems to be continuing in Bristol Township as a permanent installation in spite of the efforts of extremists.

Human relations training and better understanding and communications among groups and individuals cannot alone solve the problems of an age of rebellion. Lives must be protected in times of crisis. The innocent must be protected from the fanatic. Crime cannot go unpunished. On the other hand, we must continue positive efforts for improvement. As Eleanor Roosevelt said, "It is better to light one little candle than to curse the darkness."

9

> When policies are positively stated in terms of desirable purposes, we see a dynamic school district. When the regulations are humane and democratic, we see a district where law is the servant rather than the master of the staff.
>
> **Larson and McGoldrick** [1]

Policies and Regulations Affecting Discipline

The disciplinary problems of a school or school district are usually reflected in its written policies, procedural guidelines, regulations, and by-laws. Usually the district with the most problems is the one with the most policies and regulations related to discipline. Ironically, it is also usually the district with the most severe prescribed punishment for disciplinary violations!

In spite of ample lessons of history, some educators still seem to feel that disciplinary problems can almost always be

---

[1] Knute Larson and James McGoldrick, *Handbook of School Letters* (West Nyack, New York, Parker Publishing Company, Inc., 1970), p. 173.

Policies and Regulations Affecting Discipline   141

solved by escalating the swiftness and severity of punishment. When, for instance, student demonstrations get out of hand, we have recently seen the use of military force. Where will that end? Machine guns mounted on the campus? The Boston Massacre began with a demonstration against repressive measures. In spite of a record that shows that restraint was exercised by the soldiers, that incident will never be forgotten.

As indicated in Chapter 5, recent years have seen a far-reaching change in the attitudes and actions of our courts on matters of school discipline. American courts, especially at the higher levels, have made it very clear that the public schools do not have supreme authority over students. They never have, in fact, had such authority, but in the past they frequently assumed it without too much opposition. The greater part of a principal's strength flowed from powers he did not have but which most students and parents *thought* he had!

Although the Supreme Court has, for at least a half century, taken the position that students and teachers retain all their Constitutional rights when they are in a public school, lower courts have been unwilling to interfere with disciplinary procedures, and as long as punishment was not cruel or unusual, the courts generally supported the schools.

Has there been, as some teachers feel, a complete reversal of position in our courts? Are the courts, as some administrators feel, trying to take over the operation of our schools? To both questions I sincerely feel that the answer is no. A careful analysis of recent court decisions, some of which contradict each other, reveals a movement toward the elimination of arbitrary judgment in the administration of school discipline. A firm anchor remains, however, in the troubled waters. *The rights of the individual cease when their exercise interferes with the educative process.* No student, in other words, has the right to interfere with the education of other students. A reasonable interpretation must, of course, be made of this broad guideline. No court will accept the notion that anything a student does that irritates a teacher is interfering with education. On the other hand, extremely bizarre clothing style certainly will distract attention in the classroom. As has always been the case, good common sense must prevail in school discipline today.

School principals, especially at the secondary level, are facing extremely trying times. Militancy and activism may fluctuate in intensity, but there is no indication of any return to any (real or imagined) good old days. More trying times lie ahead. Principals who escalate petty tyranny will not survive. Principals who recognize that basic citizenship rights and responsibilities belong in our schools and that reasonable activism is a legitimate means of hastening reform, will not only survive, but probably succeed.

A POSITIVE APPROACH

All policies and regulations of schools and school districts should be carefully reviewed in the light of recent court decisions and increasing student militancy. A minimal reason would be to avoid expensive and time-consuming legal actions. A more important reason would be to extend basic American justice to all according to current interpretations of the Constitution of the United States.

Broad participation is essential to an orderly and sensible review of existing policies and regulations. In addition to teachers, administrators, and board members, responsible and mature students should be involved, particularly in the review of school regulations. All participants should be carefully briefed, preferably by an attorney, on recent court decisions concerning the operation of schools. This will take time and, perhaps, money. The effort will be extremely worthwhile, not only because of the creation of just and meaningful policies and regulations, but because the participants will gain real insights into the substance of justice and law.

A few guidelines can be developed, with the assistance of an attorney, to use as a yardstick to measure policies and regulations. Most school policies and regulations fall into a few broad categories:

1. Requiring certain actions of all or some students and/or school employees.
2. Forbidding certain actions for all or some students and/or school employees.
3. Making certain actions optional.
4. Establishing punishment for certain types of action.

Policies and Regulations Affecting Discipline 143

One way to organize such guidelines is to prepare a list of questions to apply to each policy or regulation. The following list is a sample of questions which may be used. It is not intended to be comprehensive:

1. If it is a policy, does it spell out its purpose?
2. If it is a regulation, is it based on a policy?
3. Does the policy cite its basis in law or court precedent? (See sample flag salute policy below.)
4. Is it legal under local ordinances and state laws? (I have seen many illegal school regulations.)
5. Is it based on the improvement of education? If it forbids an action, is the reason spelled out that the action would interfere with the educative process?
6. Is it as precise as possible?
7. Does it violate due process of law under the Fourteenth Amendment?
8. Does it deny anyone his rights guaranteed under the Bill of Rights?
9. Is it necessary in the first place, or was it created to solve the problems of the weakest teachers? Was it created to limit the irrational behavior of a small minority of immature and/or emotionally unstable students? Will it limit the freedom of the responsible majority in order to contain the minority (e.g., special slips to go to lavatory, library, etc.)?
10. Is it reasonable and proper?

Most older policies dating back 20 or more years will probably have to be replaced or radically changed. Age has no intrinsic value in policies or regulations. Quite the opposite. Sometimes, however, very recent policies can be outdated by a court decision. The following policy on the flag salute ceremony was presented early in 1970 to the Educational Cabinet (an elected body of teachers and administrators charged with making policy recommendations to the School Board) of the Bristol Township School District in Pennsylvania. Soon after the policy was recommended, a court decision in New York set a precedent that no student could be forced to salute the flag, nor could he be required to leave the room or to be set apart in any manner while other students were performing the ceremony. If this de-

Proposed Policy*

Ceremonies and Observances—The Flag Salute Ceremony

Love and respect for our nation and for its traditions can be expressed in many ways. The observance of traditional ceremonies is one. Good citizenship is another. Lawful dissent against institutional imperfections is yet another. A desire to improve the institutions of a free nation is inherent in good citizenship. The right to hold unpopular opinions in the pursuit of this desire is one of the grateful acknowledgments made by the American when he salutes his flag.

He also salutes many other things, such as the sacrifices of many generations of Americans who have also sought to improve our nation. Perhaps his most significant acknowledgment is the implication of gratitude for his basic rights and freedoms, which are limited only by the rights and freedoms of each one of his fellow Americans.

The Laws of the Commonwealth of Pennsylvania provide that all schools, public or private, 'shall establish and direct the conduct of appropriate daily instruction of, in lieu thereof, at least one full period per week, for the purpose of affirming and developing allegiance to and respect for the flag of the United States of America, and for the promoting of a clear understanding of our American way of life, with all of the unparalleled individual opportunities, and our republican form of government, with its responsiveness to majority decisions and demands.'

The Board of School Directors has chosen the option of a daily ceremony of pledging allegiance to the flag, but does not in so choosing absolve the professional staff from a responsibility of providing appropriate instruction to students in the understanding of and a respect for the traditions and the laws of the nation represented by that flag. The Board feels that students must learn as early as possible why they salute the flag and what the flag represents. It is considered desirable but not adequate in itself to teach the students the meaning of the words in the pledge. Students

---

* Note: See Chapter 11, "Action," item 7, under *Policies and Regulations* for a more recent development with respect to this policy.

Policies and Regulations Affecting Discipline

must also learn to understand the deeper meanings of the words and the ceremony. This concern and this intent of the Board shall be reflected in the curriculum of the Bristol Township School District at appropriate places and levels and by an indication of appropriate methods.

A Supreme Court ruling of 1944 established that when a school district chooses to observe the flag salute ceremony, all students (except foreign nationals) must participate unless they are members of a recognized religious group whose tenets specifically forbid the ceremony.

The flag salute controversy deserves special attention because it has been the source of many emotional reactions. It is perfectly reasonable to expect our schools to teach patriotism, to encourage students to love their land. Too often, however, this job is handled badly or not at all, as in the cases of our Pledge of Allegiance to the Flag and our National Anthem. I recently questioned a number of high school students concerning the "pledge." Not one could recall ever having been instructed in the meaning or the significance of the words. A few recalled having the words defined for them as in an English lesson, but none recalled any discussion about the why or what of this familiar ceremony. This was the reason behind the introduction of the policy question to the Educational Cabinet. Wide differences exist among educators concerning patriotism ranging from "my country can do no wrong" to "I love my country. That's why I want to improve it by radical changes."

I believe it is necessary to examine carefully the phrase in our Pledge of Allegiance that says, "One nation, under God, *with liberty and justice for all.*" Is it not conceivable that an American Indian, a Mexican-American, or a black American can love his land and still be convinced that "liberty and justice for all" is simply not a fact in his life? Is it not conceivable that he cannot in honesty utter words which he knows to be untrue? Would it not be an act of honesty officially to reword this passage, stating it as a *goal* rather than as a *fact?* Has any nation, anywhere, at any time ever truly provided "liberty and justice" for *all?* This would not eliminate the objections of the troublemaker but it would answer the complaint of the truly honest objector.

SAMPLE POLICIES AND REGULATIONS

Constitutional Guarantees to Juveniles

The following policy was developed chiefly by a pupil personnel administrator who worked with the police, the administrative staff, and a number of counselors. If it seems a trifle vague at times, it merely reflects the vagueness of a situation which has developed as a result of a number of court decisions which, themselves, have not always been crystal clear.

Where it states, for example, that "school officials shall act *in loco parentis,*" a reader may well question what this means today. The basic concept of a teacher acting in place of a parent has been challenged in many cases. In that specific school district, however, there would be very little misunderstanding on that point. It would simply mean that the administrator would act as if he were a just and reasonable parent of the student in question. He would protect the student as much as possible without interfering with the necessary process of law enforcement. Under ordinary conditions, this would mean permitting the questioning under conditions spelled out in the policy and its subsidiary regulation.

Policy 1411 [2]

As stated by the Supreme Court of the United States, juveniles, in or out of school, have the same constitutional rights as all other citizens. School district personnel must protect these rights while pupils are in their custody, and are to treat pupils accordingly.

Should law enforcement officers desire to question a pupil in school about *participation* in a criminal act, they cannot be permitted to do so unless parental permission is obtained, or there is a warrant issued for the arrest of the pupil.

Should law enforcement officers desire to question a pupil, while in the process of, but not about participation in, a criminal act, parental permission should be sought. If parental permission cannot be obtained, school officials shall act *in loco parentis.*

---

[2] *Policies, By-Laws, Regulations,* Bristol Township School District (Pennsylvania).

Policies and Regulations Affecting Discipline

Should a criminal act or suspicion of a criminal act take place on school grounds when school or school-related activities are in session, it should be brought to the immediate attention of the chief building administrator, who will investigate the situation. If this act creates immediate danger to the health and safety of anyone in the school, the principal must take whatever action is necessary to remove the threat of that danger. As soon as possible, the parents of the pupils involved and the police should be notified.

In suspected criminal cases, school employees should not search individuals or individual lockers. This should be done by law enforcement officers. However, routine inspections of lockers and facilities may be conducted by school officials in the interests of health and safety.

Whenever possible, the law enforcement officer should contact the principal by telephone before visiting the school. Whenever possible, the officers interviewing pupils during school hours shall wear plain clothes and drive unmarked cars. If the officer is unknown to the school administrator, suitable identification should be requested and presented.

Proposed Administrative Regulation 1411

A. Before students can be questioned in school about participation in a criminal act, parental permission or a warrant must be obtained. In situations of questioning during a criminal investigation (when the student being questioned is not a known participant), parental permission should be sought.

   1. Parents are to be contacted by telephone and fully advised of the situation.

   2. If possible, they should come to the school and be present during the questioning.

   3. If they cannot be present, their permission shall be requested for both the administrator and the law officer to question the student.

      a. Should the student be suspected of a criminal act, he and his parents must be informed of their rights. Every law enforcement officer has been instructed on how to do this.

      b. Notation of the above notification shall be made by the principal and placed in the confidential file. It should include the place, date,

time, and signatures of the officer and the administrator.
4. In all such cases, a school administrator must be present during the questioning. The administrator shall clarify the accusatory or investigatory nature of the questioning with the law officer prior to the questioning. The administrator will thus make certain that the student knows that he has the right to legal counsel, that he can remain silent if he wishes, and that anything he says may be used against him.

B. Policy 1411 refers to immediate danger. The following examples are cited to assist interpretation:
1. If information should be received that a bomb was in a certain locker and that it would explode in ten minutes, this must be treated as an immediate danger.
2. If, on the other hand, information is received that a student has a supply of drugs in his locker and is selling them to other students, a different situation exists. There is danger but not *immediate* danger. The principal can assign surveillance to see that no further transactions will take place. Then he would call the police, requesting that they obtain a warrant to search the suspect and his locker. (Warrants can usually be obtained quickly and easily by police officers.) This will insure that any evidence found is admissible in court. If further investigation is required, the previously stated procedures will be followed.

C. In the event it becomes necessary to make an arrest during school hours, the officer should go to the principal's office and the student should be summoned to the office. In this case, a teacher could be sent to the classroom and could accompany the student to the office.
1. The school shall then record the name and the organization of the officer, the time of the arrest, and the place to which the student was taken.
2. The school shall follow the procedure outlined in policy 1411 for contacting parents, and shall also notify police of the results of these efforts.

Discipline and Punishment

The next policy may be of interest to the reader because it applies to a district in which corporal punishment is permitted under state law and under local policies and regulations. While it has been established in precedent that a student may not be struck on the head, one ruling indicated that the judge felt that "nature had provided an appropriate place for corporal punishment." At the time of this writing, wooden paddles may still be found in the schools of Pennsylvania, usually in a drawer in the principal's desk.

This is an older policy, going back at least a decade. We note with interest the direct reference to *in loco parentis* in item 1 which sets the stage for the use of physical force as a parent would use it—"kindly and justly."

Without making a value judgment on corporal punishment, which still seems to be necessary in some places and under some conditions, this policy could stand some rewriting. Note that there is no clear separation between the use of force in preserving order (breaking up a fist fight, for example) and the use of force as *punishment*. Presumably the latter would take place after a proper investigation and in the presence of a witness.

It can hardly be argued today that a teacher should be prohibited by law from using force when necessary to defend himself, preserve order, or protect persons and property. I question, however, the use of corporal *punishment* on students over 14 years of age. It has been my experience that older students who cannot be controlled by other means have usually been subjected to a great deal of physical punishment with little or no success. They are seldom spoiled because the rod was spared. The rod has failed. Why try it again?

Policy 5144 [3]

Discipline/Punishment

   1. The professional employee has the right to exercise the same authority as to the conduct and behavior over pupils during the time they are in atten-

---

[3] *Policies, By-Laws, Regulations,* Bristol Township School District (Pennsylvania).

dance, including the time required in going to and from their homes, as the parents, guardians, or persons in parental relation to such pupils may exercise over them. (School Code, 1957, Section 1317.)

2. The professional employee is to deal kindly and justly with every pupil as an individual, without prejudice or partiality.

3. The professional employee is to respect the pupil as an individual as well as a member of a group or class.

4. The professional employee is to maintain a classroom which is conducive to teaching as well as learning, through practices which are based upon knowledge of the psychology of the age of the pupils.

5. The professional employee shall use physical force only as a last resort in the most unusual circumstances and after all other corrective measures have been used without success. Teacher, principal, guidance counselor, and other specialists shall combine their efforts to help the pupil before physical force is administered.

6. If it is practical and possible, whenever a professional employee uses physical force, another staff member should be present as a witness.

7. A professional employee may use the necessary physical force when it is essential for self-defense, the preservation of order, or the protection of other persons or property of the school district. Whenever such an occasion arises, the professional employee is to report the situation to the principal as soon as it is practical.

8. The principal or his designated representative may temporarily suspend a pupil on account of misconduct or disobedience. The principal shall promptly notify the district superintendent. No set time for suspension is permitted, and in every instance, the principal or his designated representative shall take active steps to return the pupil to school as soon as possible.

Legal Reference: Purdon's Penn St. Ann—Title 24—Education 24—Para. 13-1317. Authority of teachers, vice-principals, and principals over pupils. (As amended 1963.)

Regulation 5144

Discipline/Punishment

A pupil may be sent to the principal's office only when the continued presence of the pupil in the classroom interferes with the learning processes. When this is done, a written explanation of the reason for the referral should be made. This information is necessary so the person dealing with the referral may better understand the problem. Once referred to the principal, disposition of the case belongs to him; the teacher must be prepared to accept his solution.

Drug and Narcotics Control

Almost every American school district has done a great deal of soul searching on the narcotics problem. Teachers and administrators who face this problem are placed in a cruel and potentially dangerous position. On the one hand, they want to help the student who has fallen into the drug trap. On the other hand, they cannot break the law by failing to report a known felony. No teacher or principal enjoys the immunities of a priest, a lawyer, or a newspaperman.

To compound the dilemma, very few parents can accept the fact that *their* children might be using drugs. In spite of almost daily newspaper accounts of drug arrests involving young people from fine homes, many adults cling to the myth that narcotics abuse only takes place in city slums. When a teacher, therefore, becomes certain that a student from a prominent family is using drugs, he may think twice about informing the parents. The first backlash will almost surely be directed at the informant. Furthermore, in the student subculture, he will be viewed as a police informer and will become the target of further antagonism.

More importantly, he will no longer be "trusted" and will not be in a position to assist students who have a drug problem. This policy represents a sincere effort to deal directly with this complicated problem without placing educators in a position of complicity with law violation and without making it impossible for them to help kids in trouble.

I believe it to be a good policy which, like any good policy, must change with new conditions. I do not recommend, however, that it be transplanted as written into another school district. It may offer useful guidelines, but I feel that it is important for each district to work out its own policy and regulations on narcotics, with the help of local (and possibly state) police, with the advice of an attorney. I also feel it important to consult high school students, who usually know far more about the local drug scene than any adults in the community.

Policy 5147 [4]

1. *Suspicion of Drug Use.*

The school principal, upon establishing reason to suspect that a pupil is engaged in the illicit use of drugs, shall discuss this suspicion with the pupil in a face-to-face conference. The suspicion and the reasons for that suspicion shall be presented. The principal shall advise the pupil of the school's responsibility to share the suspicion with his parents. A conference with the parents shall be held shortly thereafter. At this conference, the principal shall (in addition to discussing the above) impress upon the parents the seriousness of the suspected behavior, and the ways of dealing with the suspected behavior and underlying causes.

2. *Suspected to Be Under the Active Influence of Drugs on School Property.*

When a student is suspected of being under the active influence of drugs while on school property, the first responsibility of the school authorities is to secure appropriate medical attention. The parents shall be telephoned immediately, advised of the symptoms observed, and asked to take the student to the family physician or the hospital.

If the parents cannot provide transportation, permission shall be secured for the school nurse-teacher and for other appropriate staff to transport the student to the physician or hospital. In either case, the receiving physician shall be informed of the symptoms observed by the school personnel. The juvenile officer will be similarly informed.

If the symptoms are considered to be so severe as to present an emergency situation, the school nurse-

---

[4] *Policies, By-Laws, Regulations,* Bristol Township School District (Pennsylvania).

teacher shall take the student immediately to the hospital while other appropriate personnel inform the parents and the family physician.

If the physician confirms that the student was actually under the influence of an illicit drug, as defined in the law, he is obligated to inform the local law enforcement authorities.

If charges are brought against the student by the policy, the administrative regulation regarding *apprehension for alleged drug abuse* shall go into effect.

If no charge is made because abuse was not confirmed by the physician but, on the basis of study by the school principal or subsequent behavior by the student, the school authorities continue to suspect drug abuse activity, the administrative regulation regarding *suspicion of drug use* shall go into effect.

3. *Suspected Possession of Drugs on School Property.*

The school principal, upon establishing reason to suspect that a student is carrying or has carried illegal drugs onto school property, shall confront the student, in a conference, with the suspicion and supporting data. The student shall be advised of the principal's obligation to inform his parents and juvenile authorities. A parent conference shall be held shortly thereafter. As it is beyond the competence and the role of any school staff member to determine the true nature of the substance in question, the parents can only be advised of the suspicion and any other data which tends to support that suspicion.

The parents shall be apprised of the drug abuse laws, and the known health and safety risks associated with drug abuse. They shall also be informed of the programs and services available for dealing with this behavior and the underlying causes.

If it is considered appropriate, on the basis of the above conference, other appropriate consultations, further substantiation of the suspicion, and/or continued suspicious behavior, the principal may invoke suspension.

4. *Suspicion of Selling or Transferring Drugs on School Property.*

In instances when a student is suspected of selling or transferring drugs on school property, the school authorities have the dual responsibility of protecting the rest of the student body from potentially dangerous influences and protecting the individual student's right to due process under the law. The policy is based upon two additional assumptions: (1) determination of the true nature of any suspicious material being passed or sold is beyond the competence of the school staff; (2) adjudicating whether the material was being ing sold or transferred is beyond the appropriate role of the school.

When the school principal has substantial reason to suspect that a student is engaged in the selling and/or transferring of drugs, the student shall be confronted in a conference with the suspicion and grounds. He shall be advised of the school's responsibility to share this suspicion with his parents. The parents shall be informed in a subsequent conference. The parents shall also be apprised that the principal is compelled, due to the seriousness of the suspected behavior, to share this suspicion with the local juvenile authorities. The parents shall be given information regarding the relevant drug abuse laws and advised to consult with their physician and attorney. The parents shall also be apprised of the various services available to them and the student. It shall also be affirmed in the parent conference that if there is any future substantial evidence of selling or transferring, then suspension may be invoked until the school authorities have reason to believe the activity will cease.

5. *Apprehended for Alleged Violation of Drug Abuse Statutes.*

When a student is apprehended and charged with a violation of the federal or state drug abuse laws, the student shall be permitted to continue attending school pending the disposition of his case by the courts. Once the school authorities are informed of a student so charged, the school principal shall initiate an evaluation of the student's school history and present functioning in school. The school authorities should be prepared to share such information, if it is requested by the court. The school authorities shall take into careful consideration any recommendations that the court may make relevant to disposition and follow-up.

The school staff shall make every effort to involve the student in appropriate rehabilitative services, prior to and following the disposition of the case.

Freedom of Speech

Many students today seem to feel that freedom of expression has become an absolute right, with no restrictions whatsoever. They need to be reminded about these restrictions. Some type of policy should be written. Here is a suggested one.

Proposed Policy

Freedom of Speech

The First Amendment of our Constitution provides for the freedom of the citizen to express his opinions. This includes opinions which may be unpopular or which may differ from those of persons in authority.

School officials shall see that these rights are protected for students and teachers. It is not true, however, that any citizen has the right to say anything he pleases, anywhere, at any time. Uncontrolled liberty is anarchy.

Freedom of speech is always limited by policies, legal considerations, and reasonable standards of good taste. In schools, it is also limited when it interferes with the educational process.

A student must also recognize that an opinion based on ignorance, bias, or incomplete knowledge cannot be as valid as an opinion based on a more complete knowledge of specific facts and on careful, thorough judgment. Unless he can understand this, he cannot understand the reason he attends school.

Disruption of School

Every district should spell out a reasonable policy to contain and control activism. While it may seem unnecessary to say that law breaking will not be tolerated, it can be very useful to record the attitude of the Board of Education on activism and on what they intend to do about it. Following such a statement, the Board can go on to regulations controlling student behavior, taking care not to violate student rights as they have been defined in court decisions.

Bristol Township, Pennsylvania, enacted such a policy in 1969:

Student Conduct: Disruption of School

It is the purpose of the Board of Education, acting within the intent and letter of the laws and constitution of this state, to provide instruction for students at public expense. Any act of any person or persons to interfere with or thwart that purpose is unlawful. Therefore, actions by a student or students to interfere materially or substantially with the operation of the school by infringing upon the rights of others to accept instruction, by defacing or destroying school property, by rioting, break-ins, sit-ins, lie-ins, smash-ins, and picketing to force students not to cross picket lines—are illegal. Students who engage in such activities will be punished to the full extent of the law.

The cited policies may or may not be easily applied to the problems of other school districts, but they should be carefully examined in terms of wording, references to law, and conformity with recent court decisions.

As I have indicated, the procedure in ordinary times is to write policies and regulations in response to actual problems, not in anticipation of problems to come. We are living in anything but ordinary times. We are living in an age of rebellion. Today it is most prudent to examine the policy responses of other districts to crises we will probably face in our district. The worst possible attitude to assume today would be, "It can't happen here!"

10

> Put them in one schoolroom—tough adolescent street fighter, hyperactive child, high achiever, low achiever—and what do you get? Chaos, ordinarily, nobody learning anything. But when the schoolroom is the big, bright Independent Learning Center at Chicago's Ray School, small miracles happen. Nervous children find peace. Tough gang leaders find something besides fighting that they can do well. High achievers go higher, and low achievers finally discover some stimulant to working and learning.
>
> **Lois Wille** [1]

Improving the Climate for Learning

If we exclude the specific problems rooted in race, poverty, unhappy homes, and the difficult life styles of urban society, we cannot help but note that a significant percentage of the remaining discipline problems in our schools are caused by a meaningless curriculum, mediocre and bad teaching, and inhumane organization in general. If we can eliminate these discipline problems through substantial reform of these elements, perhaps our schools can become places of trust and truth, happier places for everyone. One way to improve discipline is to improve instruction.

---

[1] Lois Wille, "Room for Miracles," *American Education*, August-September, 1969, 7.

Schools are like silly putty. Their organizational patterns can be stretched and shaped by creative hands. But like the amorphous glob of plastic, they have a relentless "memory" and when the creative hands are withdrawn, they tend to revert to their original shape. Perhaps we should call this the *Silly Putty Syndrome.*

Today's itinerant educational leader may change a school or a school district, but if he fails to remain for five or six years the changes may not remain. When he moves on, if he is not replaced by a like-minded individual, the syndrome may surface the moment he walks out the door. Unfortunately, it is more difficult for our poorer districts and our problem-ridden urban districts to retain strong, reform-minded executives for long. Thus schools which need reform the most are least likely to get it, and educational change becomes concentrated in our suburbs, where our best schools have been generally located since World War II.

One fact seems clear. *Substantial and lasting reforms must be made in our schools very soon.* Many of these changes involve curriculum content. For the most part, however, the most pressing need for reform is in our organizational patterns—our arrangements for learning.

Part of the problem is superficial and has to do with words such as innovative and experimental, when they are applied to ideas, arrangements, and hardware that have been successfully used for many years. Why, for example, do we give such labels to television instruction, which has been around for over two decades? Do we really need to "experiment" with a medium which has accumulated a mountain of evidence that it can be used effectively in teaching? We hardly need any experimentation or brainstorming in our classrooms today. What we need to do is *implement* ideas that have been tried and proven over and over again. Research belongs in the universities. Action belongs in the schools.

I am not attempting to say that we have had no change in the last decade in our schools. Possibly we have seen more change in the last 20 years than has been made previously since the landing of the pilgrims. But it has not taken place in areas

Improving the Climate for Learning

which need it the most. And, unfortunately, much recent reform has come and gone without taking firm root.

Two institutions have contributed greatly to recent educational reform: our federal government with its massive input of money for improvements and our graduate schools of education with their increased stewardship for ailing schools. We must observe, however, that the federal effort has not always sustained reform beyond the point where it could prosper under the care of the local district. How many promising programs were tragically abandoned when federal assistance was withdrawn and the local districts had to spend what has become known as "real money"?

It is also true that many university efforts have skipped over the ghetto problems, which so often border directly on university property and have moved out into the affluent suburbs. It is, of course, much easier to consolidate change in suburbia where the buildings are new and more flexible, where a better paid staff is available, and where there is a real chance for the community to continue to support new programs that prove effective.

Here is an instance where we can point to an example of success for the youth revolution of the late sixties. In many urban universities it was the militancy of *students* that awakened the institutions to their responsibilities to their ghetto neighbors. It was the *students* who protested the demolition of slum housing to make room for a new gym. It was the *students* who manned the storefront tutoring schools, who worked with VISTA in the ancient schoolhouses serving the ghettos.

What is needed now is a vast extension of the stewardship of both private and public sectors into reform of education. This reform movement needs to reach into every urban and rural slum, into the remote areas of our nation: into Appalachia; into rural Maine; into our Indian reservations; into our deprived coal areas; and into the mill towns with the empty factories. The alternative is a complete abandonment of our cherished concept of equality of opportunity for the children of America.

A new vehicle, a new machine for change must be created —one that borrows freely from the successful aspects of existing machinery. A new combination of forces must be aligned. We are not without models. We have the extension services of universities. We have the still controversial performance contracts of private firms moving into teaching disadvantaged children. We have many well-known consulting firms in the field and an army of consultants in all areas. We need to consolidate our efforts, to create an educational army to fight the war against ignorance and poverty in the midst of plenty.

NEEDED—AN AUXILIARY ADMINISTRATIVE UNIT

Let us consider one possible way to organize our efforts in educational reform. Two major problems faced by most districts which desire to make changes may be summarized quite briefly:

1. There is no source of sufficient money.
2. Existing personnel are either already overworked and/or not suitably trained to carry out the initial tasks involved in effecting substantial changes.

To solve these problems, one must first find sources of funds. These must probably be the usual ones—the federal government and/or private foundations. Since both of these institutions have already demonstrated a great interest in improving our public schools, it would seem reasonable that they would be at least open minded about a new and better way of reaching that goal. With proper leadership, the prestige of a university graduate school, and an intelligently conceived and well-written proposal, at least seed money should be attainable.

The second problem is far easier to deal with. An adequate group of people, well-trained and experienced in the dynamics of change would be assigned to an auxiliary administrative unit that would attach itself to the administration of a school district until a specific reform is firmly rooted in that district. This could take months or years. The unit could either be gradually withdrawn or totally withdrawn at a given time.

This unit could be created in the private or public sector or in combination. It seems logical to me, however, that the sponsorship should at least initially come from a graduate school of education. What is needed is a moon shot approach, staffed by the best qualified people wherever they can be found.

Certain features that must be built into such an organization are obvious. Others are not and would surface as a result of experience. Some of the more obvious would be:

1. A contractual relationship with a school district with exact specifications as to what is to be accomplished, how it is to be accomplished, when it is to be started, and when it is to be finished. Also, of course, a projection will be necessary to spell out future costs to the district in terms of personnel, space, hardware, and software, to sustain the reform.
2. Sufficient funds, committed in advance to cover the costs until the district takes over.
3. A provision for follow-up "booster shots" after the withdrawal of the auxiliary unit.
4. A statement of relationship between the unit and the district which gives the unit enough authority to proceed with minimal interference with the regular operations of the district.
5. A provision for release time as necessary for the in-service education of the district staff. This must be handled carefully because it can lead to much difficulty and poor public relations.
6. A provision for adequate dissemination of public information and the preparation of parents and students for the change.
7. Authority vested in the administration of the unit to obtain the necessary personnel from whatever source is available (not just from the sponsoring institution). This freedom to hire and dismiss purely on the basis of effectiveness could be the single greatest advantage of this unit over conventional educational groupings of manpower.

One of the benefits of this or any new and systematic approach to effecting change would be to cut down on the considerable duplication of creative efforts in our school districts. Innovation in schools today can best be described as chaotic, for too many teachers are wasting precious time in reinventing the wheel and struggling with tasks that have already been completed in other districts.

THE ORDERING OF GOALS

Major thrusts for change today seem to fall into a few broad categories:
1. Relating curriculum organization and content to a *now generation* and to the emerging problems they will live with in the twenty-first century.
2. The individualization of instruction. We have talked and talked about individual differences for decades. We have done very little about it other than to gradually reduce teaching loads on the assumption that individualized education would result.

Today we are taking a new look at the importance of what each student *already knows* before we expose him to a learning experience, to the student's *rate of learning,* and to his *style of learning.* More importantly, we are beginning to learn how to harness the computer to help us with this enormous task.

One of the more promising breakthroughs in this area is the project known as *Individually Prescribed Instruction or IPI.* This system generates a vast amount of knowledge about each student. This is used daily by the teacher in preparing prescriptions for each student's learning experiences. The computer and systems analysis are part of the procedure along with very elaborate testing.

This project has been criticized as being far too elaborate and expensive for broad application in our schools. It seems very early, however, to make these judgments. The development of any prototype is expensive. Refinements will appear in due time. If IPI does nothing more than improve our testing machinery, it will be well worth the effort.

Individualized instruction requires more than a plan. It requires appropriate space, apart from the library and classrooms. The quotation at the beginning of this chapter is from an article describing such a center in a Chicago elementary school. At the time it was written, the project was limited to one building. Predictably, the cost of staffing was high (a six to one ratio), but the results seemed to be startling. The cost of maintaining people in specialized residential institutions can run as high as $10,000 per person. It would seem that preventive medicine is far cheaper.

Improving the Climate for Learning

3. The removal of grade barriers and the substitution of continuous progress for each child according to his own learning rate and learning style.

At one time or another, each of us was probably admonished in school not to read such and such a book because it was material to be used in the next grade. Most teachers tried to enrich the materials for brighter students but the grade barrier was very real when it came to moving ahead in the basic curriculum. For many years now, extensive efforts have been made to reduce or remove these barriers from K-12. Organizational problems are great, especially in smaller schools, but there is now no lack of know-how. Schools have been built to accommodate such a program. The implementation work of Frank Brown and Sidney Rollins in the secondary level has had a noteworthy impact on our schools as has the efforts of Goodlad and Anderson at the elementary level.

The triple thrust in curriculum relevance, individualized instruction, and continuous progress would seem to me to give us all the challenge we need in educational innovation for many years to come. If we can master the nuts and bolts of these movements and extend them throughout our schools, discipline problems would be substantially removed.

THE EMERGENCE OF ACCOUNTABILITY THROUGH BETTER DATA PROCESSING

Public schools have always been held accountable to the taxpayers, but in the past it has mainly been a nickle-nursing, parsimonious accountability based solely on strong motivation to keep taxes low. It was not an accountability based on a desire for effective improvement in instruction. Today the public is demanding answers to new questions:

1. How much does each specific program cost?
2. How effective is each program in relationship to its cost?
3. How can we improve each program most economically and effectively?
4. What will each reform cost in the initial stage? How much each year thereafter? How and when will it be evaluated?

Accountability and a more sophisticated use of far more accurate data seem to be going hand in hand. The utilization of computers in program planning and budgeting is increasing rapidly, particularly in larger districts. Through an integrated system of data processing, accurate budget projections can be made in all areas of the curriculum and projected programs can be simulated in advance.

The computer has already become slightly controversial in America. It has gathered around it the usual cult of enthusiasts who view it as anything from an indispensable tool to the ultimate solution to our problems. They rush to its defense when it seems to err. "Garbage in—garbage out," they say. The machine is only as good as the input. But they have largely ceased to claim that it will cut costs by doing the work of many clerks. It has become clear that this saving is offset by our growing appetite for more and more information. When it becomes clear that the machine can tell us how many blue-eyed students in California failed home economics last year, there always seems to be some zealous researcher who wants the information. Thus the introduction of computer service in a school district will almost invariably *increase* the need for clerical personnel! Administrators take note.

On the other side of the argument are people who are suspicious to antagonistic. Some are simply unwilling to take the time or expend the energy to learn what the monster can and cannot do. Others fear the growing sacredness of the machine in American life. They fear the moment when a definitive argument is worded, "We can't introduce that new program. The computer says it will cost too much."

Somewhere between these positions, of course, lies a reasonable attitudinal area. We know that data processing has taken us from the primitive pen and paper days through the manual ice pick routine into computerized scheduling in our secondary schools. We know that it has improved the efficiency of our business operations. We know that computer-linked improvements are well on the way in classroom instruction. When costs are reduced and when instructional and testing software is improved, broad acceptance will follow.

The Program Planning Budgeting System has made possible far more intelligent problem solving in many areas. We know that California, after a difficult period of several years, has coordinated a statewide data processing system. If such a large and diverse state can achieve uniformity in counseling records, etc., how long will it be before we have a nationwide data processing system in education? Resisting this movement would be as effective as trying to stop the rising of tomorrow's sun. We had better learn to use this awakening giant as a servant of education and not let it become our master.

ORGANIZING OUR SCHOOLS

In spite of increasing financial problems (and sometimes in an effort to solve them), organizational plans involving extended commitments for the schools are being considered with increased interest and seriousness. Each, I believe, has a potential for the improvement of discipline through a more meaningful program. Some of these are:

The Extended School Year

We have been concerned in American education for about a half century with our wasteful schedule of approximately 180 days per year and the learning loss which takes place during the long summer vacation. We have also been concerned about the high cost of school construction which has soared in the past few years. Industry is concerned with summer inefficiency due to the loss of key senior employees who prefer to take their vacation in the summer when the kids are out of school. Many students are concerned about the intense competition for summer jobs among students. Why doesn't something happen on a broad scale?

Here and there things have been happening for a long time, since the early twenties. Things are happening now on a broad scale, in the Metropolitan Atlanta area. From the time Aliquippa, Pennsylvania went on a quarter plan with a year-around operation to avoid spending a large sum on new construction (this lasted until 1938 when money became available), until 1968 when Fulton County, Georgia began an urban-suburban coordinated year-around plan, we have learned a great deal about this promising idea. Perhaps the most intensive work being done at this time is in the Research Office of the New York State Department of Education and by the strongest voice being raised today in favor of the plan, that of Dr. George Thomas of that office.

His office has come up with a variety of plans and a wide spectrum of findings and opinions. He supports the idea of many other pioneers in the field that you should not sell the idea on the basis of saving money. Unless the curriculum is changed and arrangements for learning are altered to take full advantage of the plan, not very much is accomplished. These things cost money. There is a saving, of course, in the avoidance or delay of a building project. As was the case in Aliquippa, this is usually a delay. Delays of buildings today mean that you get less building for more money.

Atlanta has not sold the idea as a money saver. It costs more, they say, but you get more. In their case, the "more" includes a meaningful, regular school program in the summer for a large number of city youngsters. This is, indeed, a plus!

A summary of pro and con arguments may be summarized as follows:

1. To avoid a building program and to save money. (This is largely discredited by educational leaders of the movement, but it still motivates tax-conscious citizens.)
2. To make better use of present facilities, to minimize overcrowded conditions, and to open up areas for team teaching and individualized study.
3. To pay teachers more by having them work a longer year, thus permitting each teacher to handle a larger number of students. (This is not universally supported by teachers.)
4. To foster continuous progress for all, to enrich the rapid learner, and to help the slow learner.
5. To permit people the opportunity to take vacations in off-seasons and thus save money. (A widespread adoption could also mean a lengthening of profitable seasons for traditional summer tourist centers, such as Maine, Cape Cod, and the New Jersey shore.)
6. To permit industry to maintain year-around efficiency by a better spacing of vacations for skilled workers.

The disadvantages are more difficult to summarize. Some things can be nailed down, but others are rooted in attitudes and fear of change. We can say, for example, that:

1. Custodial costs will be higher and maintenance schedules more difficult to manage.
2. Teachers will have no opportunity for summer study and travel to improve their effectiveness.
3. Bussing costs will be higher.
4. Students who transfer to and from districts with a conventional year will experience difficulties.
5. Many schools will have to be air conditioned to make them tolerable for use in the summers.
6. Sports seasons would be difficult to maintain.

On the other hand, attitudes are difficult to assess. A substantial number of teachers were motivated to enter the profession at least partially by the attraction of the 180-day year. They are not enthralled by losing it nor are they convinced that the old resistance to higher salaries because of a short year will be eliminated by the change. There is substantial evidence that there will still be resistance to higher teacher salaries, even if the "long vacation" is eliminated.

It is true that most graduate schools are geared to the teachers' summer vacation. If a widespread change takes place, however, the graduate schools will have to fall in line. It is also true that many military reserve organizations are set up to perform most of their two-week training sessions in the summers due to large numbers of students and educators involved. They, too, can change. It would probably improve their overall program.

Many feel that most resistance to this change comes from superintendents and other administrators. But these leaders are gradually becoming more sensitive to the needs of students. It seems clear to me that the year-around schools will become better places for students (if they are air conditioned). Many colleges have already made the move to year-around operations.

In my opinion, the year-around school must become a reality in the near future. Action must be taken, however, on a broad basis, preferably by states or large metropolitan areas. In this way the fullest possible benefits will accrue to all, especially to industry and resort areas tied to a one-season vacation tradition. Unfortunately this would involve agreement among many independent governing bodies, preferably not only on the concept itself, but on a specific approach to it that would eliminate most, if not all of the opposition to the year-around school.

The Extended School Day

Most of our high schools conduct their basic functions between 8 A.M. and 3 P.M. Activities and sports take over until, perhaps, 5 P.M., at which time various types of adult programs move in. Even when these programs lead to a diploma they are not often correlated with the regular day program, especially in terms of hours of instruction per week, semester, and year. Nor are day students encouraged to transfer to the evening program. It is felt, with some justification, that this can become a step toward dropping out. The diploma-seeking adult who stays with the evening program has usually been out of school for some time.

A great many discipline problems in high school are traceable directly to a bad program for terminal students combined with a too-lengthy day. When kids fail in school, we often give them more of the same stuff they have already rejected. When, for example, a regional vocational school shares time with a local high school, we often find students behaving quite differently in the vocational segment than in the academic segment. In this case, the high school administrator must sometimes threaten withdrawal of the student from the vocational experience in order to get him to behave acceptably during his academic phase! It would be wrong to assume that these students do not need the academic work. Of course they do, but one questions whether they can tolerate double doses on a six-hour daily basis. The same is even more evident in the case of the terminal student who is not accepted at the vocational school, and especially if he is not enrolled in a work-experience program. Almost any change would be an improvement in his case.

One possibility would be to have overlapping shorter sessions in the late afternoon and early evening and to tie the program directly into the adult school. In this way, greater opportunities would be created for part-time work for these young people. Two students, for example, could share one job. Divested of study halls and activities which many of these youngsters reject, the school day could be shortened appreciably.

Arguments can be made that the real answer is a *longer* and *more meaningful* day. I agree, but I have heard this argument for so many years and have seen so little real improvement for the *non-college, non-vocational school,* reluctant student, that I think it is time something was done *now*. On the other hand, I have seen so much success with the simple process of fitting a job to a student so that he can learn something he considers practical, so that he can take pride in earning money, so that he can understand adult responsibility, that I must conclude that there is some special magic in *a job*.

Coaches and directors of other activities need not argue the merits of their offerings. When students want to participate, they should. When they refuse to, we must find something else for them. Otherwise, we had better prepare to let them walk out the door. Our notion that the public school can be of service to all kids at all times is presumptuous to say the least. I often feel that a sabbatical year at the age of 16 might benefit many students, especially if they were exposed to a meaningful job for that year. When the dropouts return, they are frequently more successful in school. We must also recognize the fact that in spite of our times of affluence, many adolescents must work to assist their families or to provide themselves with clothing and pocket money. The schools should help them, not hinder them in meeting this need. One way to do this would be to accommodate the schedule to the student, not vice versa.

WORK-EXPERIENCE EXTENSIONS

We have heard a great deal in recent years about the extension of the school campus into museums, libraries, industrial plants, and other resource locations of the community. We also hear occasional reports of special problems caused by the rather significant freedom of choice extended to youngsters in these programs. Now and then we hear of a rather spectacular failure.

I would prefer to limit myself here to that type of campus extension that places a student on a job for a portion of his school day, under the supervision of the school, with pay for his work and school credit for the total experience. When he is in school (mornings, alternate days, or alternate weeks), he receives his required academic work plus a job-related course taught by the work-experience supervisor.

There are many variations on this type of program in many American high schools. I have seen great successes in several schools over two decades. In every case, the success has been directly attributable to the dedicated men and women who supervised these youngsters, day after day in the field, and patiently guided them through failure to success. It is no great feat in education to come up with an idea. It is something else to make it work and continue to work, year after year. The amazing thing to me is that there are still so many schools in which no effort has been made in this direction. The formula is quite simple:

1. Hire a teacher who has more than a part-time or summer acquaintance with industrial and/or business employment.
2. Budget his salary and travel expenses so that he can: (a) visit schools in which successful programs are rooted, study these programs, and borrow any materials and information they will supply; (b) make extensive contacts in local industry and business, first at the top level, then at the personnel management level, and later at the level of the immediate supervisor who will be working with youngsters. The principal and superintendent should be involved in these contacts. A special luncheon for prospective employers is usually an effective way to begin.
3. Prepare a public information program through all possible media to inform everyone of what is really going to happen.
4. Start the entire process at least one semester before the actual beginning of the program. It is especially important to begin recruiting students early.
5. Plan a special evening assembly program for prospective students, parents, and employers.
6. In the meantime, research thoroughly all pertinent labor ordinances. Prepare the necessary papers and waivers in advance. Make up a brochure for prospective employers, outlining briefly all legal positions to be considered.

7. Discuss the whole matter in detail with top local labor leaders. If possible, get their approval. It has been my experience that labor leaders favor programs of this type if it can be established that no jobs will be lost by union members.
8. Have the teacher prepare an in-school related course which will depend upon the type of program projected. If the program is to be specialized, e.g. nurses' aides, restaurant training, supermarket training, distributive education, etc., it will be easier to do. If the program is to encompass a wide variety of jobs, broad matters such as labor-management relations should be featured.
9. Give the teacher a reasonable work load so that he can visit each student and his supervisor on a regular basis. Depending on the distances involved, 50 students per teacher may be the breaking point. Beyond that a second supervisor should be employed. The second person may not have to be a certified teacher as long as the original teacher retains the responsibility for the classroom instruction.

Among the more successful programs of work experience I have seen in action are the following:

1. *A nurses' aide program* involving two alternating two-week periods in the hospital and in the school. The program went far beyond the basic training most aides receive, encompassing the entire senior year, and it opened up a wide variety of hospital-related employment for the students.
2. *Distributive education.* This is one of the best organized and most successful types of work experience. Almost all educators are familiar with it. Usually it also involves the operation of a school store.
3. *Clerical training.* This is of chief value for business students who do not go on to higher levels of attainment in stenography or bookkeeping. (However, the latter two areas also are well suited for work-experience programs.)
4. *Supermarket training.* Here the difficulty lies in: (a) identifying youngsters who really want careers rather than casual employment in supermarkets, and (b) freeing them for work in the mornings when they will have an opportunity to observe and learn the behind-the-scenes operations.
5. *Restaurant training.* Here the teachers' cafeteria becomes the training laboratory for beginners. Later they can be placed in local restaurants.

6. *Special-education training.* There are many jobs suitable for students with various learning disabilities. These slower learners often become valuable, loyal employees who will be inclined to remain on a job once they have mastered it. Hospitals and other institutions have many openings of this type. These youngsters respond dramatically to a successful experience in learning.

In conclusion, I wish to emphasize that the presence of an area vocational school or a vocational program within a school does not necessarily solve the problems of the terminal student. The most dramatic and intensive effort I have seen in meeting the needs of terminal students took place a few years ago in Mineola, Long Island. The comprehensive 1700-student high school had internal vocational programs in industrial electronics and auto mechanics. It was also served by a fine County Vocational-Technical school. Its industrial arts program was organized on an industrial materials and methods basis, and the students did actual production work in cooperation with a special business administration class which was geared to the problems of small business.

In addition to this, the full-time *assistant principal for terminal education* developed five separate work experience programs to serve terminal students. None of this was done at the expense of academic programs for college preparatory students wherein a high level of achievement was maintained. A progressive superintendent worked with an enlightened board to do the job right. These programs did not solve all the discipline problems of the school, but they certainly contributed enormously to alleviating the ones that were rooted in educational offerings.

STAFFING OUR SCHOOLS

Our tremendous advances in the technology of education have brought us to the brink of a new era for American teachers. The developers of educational hardware and software have demonstrated that communication with students can be accomplished much more effectively by machines than by teachers talking to kids. Thus the teacher will not become obsolete, but will assume a far more important and sophisticated role as a prescriber and manager of learning experience. She will, of course, retain her guidance and supportive role but she will command a wide variety of mechanical and human resources to assist her with her important tasks.

While we have seen differences in models developed, there seems to be no question about the implications for staffing our schools. We will certainly need, for example, more specialists in the machinery of education, more specialists in various learning disabilities, more clerical assistance, more laboratory technicians. On the other side of the coin, we will also need fewer (but better compensated) teachers.

Differentiated staffing, as this phenomenon has come to be called, involves more than simply employing fewer teachers and more non-teaching personnel. Although the developing theories differ, a great deal of attention has been given to a differentiation in assignments and salary within the teaching group itself. Teachers have long fought the concept of merit rating on the grounds that we cannot effectively measure good teaching. This may or may not be true, but to simply set a dollar value on a given qualitative measurement of performance is too simplistic an approach to be taken seriously. The teachers have been correct in their stance on conventional merit rating.

Today, however, we are beginning to theorize about differences between teachers which can be measured—some of them very easily and very accurately. The length of the teacher's day and year, for example, can be defined and measured beyond dispute. Every school district has needs for teacher time beyond the regular day and the regular year. Extensive curriculum planning, for example, requires many hours of meetings and workshops. Some good teachers prefer not to be involved. Others do. The union concept of overtime pay is hardly appropriate in a profession. Why not identify a number of eight-to-four, 11-month positions to accomplish this work? Then we could prepare job descriptions, advertise the positions (after school board authorization), and fill them.

The same can be said for a variety of needed functions: team leadership, consultation to teachers in various areas, hardware expertise, consultation on television teaching and the use of it, etc. It would not be too difficult to prepare a variety of positions of this type and align them with professional growth and ascending financial rewards. In this way, we could hopefully keep our best teachers where they belong—in the classroom. Today they can usually only be rewarded by moving them out of the classroom into some form of administration. It is almost axiomatic that a good teacher with a good lesson equals maximal learning and good *discipline*.

Perhaps we should look for the leadership in the move toward differentiated staffing from the institutions which prepare teachers. In the present period of serious oversupply of teachers in many areas, would it not make them more employable to be prepared to teach in schools organized for tomorrow as well as schools organized for yesterday?

INNOVATION AND DISCIPLINE

We have broadly covered some current trends in school organization. The unifying element seems to be greater freedom of choice and movement for students. Experienced educators know that with greater freedom comes greater problems of accounting and control, especially at the secondary level. The assumption is correctly made, in my opinion, that if it is properly handled, greater freedom will eliminate many problems of discipline which were rooted in the lock-step repression of yesterday's schools. We must also realize that the same minority of irresponsible and/or disturbed students for whom all the petty rules were created will still be with us. Will they respond positively to the new freedom? Probably not.

The simple matter of knowing where students are (or ought to be) cannot be dismissed as irrelevant or unimportant. Computer scheduling can provide the information, but teachers must still take attendance and class cutters must still be punished. Nothing embarrasses a principal as much as not being able to locate a student when he is needed for an emergency at home, especially if he is where he is supposed to be and the *system* has failed!

Modular scheduling and open campus arrangements, wherein a student may have two or more choices of locations

Improving the Climate for Learning

when he is not assigned to a class, lead to certain problems which must be solved:

1. Cutting classes, intentionally or through confusion, will increase.
2. A certain number of students will be walking the corridors at almost any given time.

The solutions may be simply stated. Enforcing them is something else:

1. Teachers must be assigned to patrol corridors as in the past. More coverage will be needed but students need not be challenged for passes. Safety supervision *must* be maintained, however.
2. Teachers must take attendance carefully and regularly and reports of cuts must be processed.
3. Students who cannot tolerate freedom must be contained within a rigid schedule and in quiet study halls with conventional supervision.
4. Some of the burden of control should be handled by the student body itself.

We must bear in mind that even in a completely conventional secondary school, laxity can lead to chaos. Corridor wandering and illegal smoking are not simply the characteristics of an innovative school. An old-fashioned sense of responsibility on the part of every teacher for the welfare and safety of students is still the only secret weapon to combat anarchy in our schools.

11

> Our bias, it should be emphasized, was not that everything now being done is necessarily wrong; it was simply that everything now being done needs to be questioned.
>
> Charles E. Silberman [1]

Action Review

EVIDENCE, RATIONALE, ACTION

I have attempted an overview of the increasingly complex problems of school discipline in an age of confrontation and revolt. It is admittedly subjective because the purpose of the book is to provide practical assistance for the harassed school administrator who must act, again and again, in the midst of crisis. My viewpoint is his viewpoint, not that of an introspective theorist who sits on solid ground, far from the epicenter of the earthquake.

---

[1] Silberman, Charles E., *Crisis in the Classroom: The Remaking of American Education* (New York, Random House, 1970), p. 4.

Today's administrator must often act quickly to solve new and crucial problems which have no precedent in his experience. He must therefore prepare himself in advance by a three-step process *before* the crisis occurs: (1) An examination and an *interpretation of evidence* will enable him to understand (not necessarily approve) what is going on among our nation's young today. (2) Having seen the evidence, he must *accept* it as a fact of his life and prepare a *rationale* for future action that includes at least a critical questioning of past actions. (3) Then he must move into positive and courageous *action* to solve the problems.

Is There a Youth Revolution?

We hardly need to list the evidence that America's youth is greatly impatient with the implementation of *reform*. Whether or not it is a *revolution* is a nice question of semantics. The *action* of youth varies from destruction and killing to peaceful protest. At its root it is not evil, but solid and simplistic idealism, based not on the invention of *new* ideas, but on a serious desire to do something about *old* ideas—like peace and love and a decent style of life for all men.

It is recorded that the actions of youth have been directed against all institutions of society. Notable among these is the institution with which the young are most familiar—our schools. There is substantial evidence that the young will not "get over" their zeal when they mature. Young professionals moving into their late twenties have not donned the grey flannel suits of the mind. They are convinced that the Biblical season has come for reshaping society and they want to remain active in the movement. Today's youth movement is not a mammoth pep rally. It is serious and will continue to be serious.

We must *accept* the basic core of idealism in the youth rebellion (or reform movement). We must accommodate it, not crush it. Wherein its goals are similar to ours, we must find ways to join it. We must understand its formless nature and try to give it form. We must join hands with the young, minimize the overstated generation gap, and find ways to make our schools into *reconstructionist* institutions that work to improve society, not ones that help young people adjust themselves to its imperfections.

Action

1. A change of attitude is an action. Our first action must be to rid ourselves of our formidable defensive attitude, put away our whitewash brushes, and honestly admit the imperfections in our schools.
2. We must stop blaming others and direct ourselves to the rapid reform of matters within our control.
3. We must immediately adopt procedures, particularly in discipline, which will rehumanize the schools and recognize the dignity of the individual student.
4. Above all, we must learn to *listen* to youth actively. Having listened, we must act on their reasonable suggestions and supply reasonable and truthful answers for matters upon which we cannot act.

Schools must not be battlegrounds. They must be places of *trust and truth*.

Militancy and Discipline

Studies in the late sixties made it clear that college-type militancy was moving down into secondary schools. Since that time, shifts of emphasis have been in evidence. Minority groups, for example, have become more radicalized and have weakened the voices of their moderates. High school radicals have become less imitative of their older brethren and have developed their own style. A perceptible generation gap has appeared between high school youth and college youth, especially in our cities.

Secondary school radicalism will vary in differing communities. An increase of violence will probably take place wherever identifiable minority groups (Negroes, Chicanos, Indians, etc.) exist in substantial numbers. Honest efforts to accommodate earlier demands, such as more minority teachers, minority studies, etc., will not satisfy the now dominant extremist factions. Sincere reform in disciplinary procedures and school organization will probably ameliorate differences between suburban educators and students and redirect the student thrusts to other agencies of society. A root cause of all of these manifestations of unrest is a strong *credibility gap* between students and educators and a lack of effective means of communication.

Confrontation tactics, ranging from riots to boycotts,

strikes, seizure of spaces, and slowdowns have become popular because the record shows that *they have been more effective* than "going through channels." The underground press has reared its sometimes ugly head in our public schools. Vandalism and sabotage are common, especially in our cities. Action must be taken *before* the crisis develops.

Action

1. In my opinion, the first action that must be taken in any public school is to reject completely the notion that *"It can't happen here."* It can. It probably will. Why not be prepared?
2. Examine the brief suggestions for handling each of the various manifestations of protest listed in Chapter 2. They are drawn from the recommendations of teachers and administrators who have experienced the various phenomena, and from the direct experience of the author. In varying degrees, they have been helpful. There is no panacea for confrontation and revolt.
3. Communications in all directions *must* be improved in all our schools. Here is where we must heed the strictures of critics who insist that *all* of our practices and organizational elements must be questioned seriously. Positively oriented organizations such as PTA's and Student Councils serve a useful purpose, but they have failed generally as avenues of communications with angry dissidents. Good communications begin with the assumption that you are communicating with the right people.
4. When the safety of people is threatened, it becomes a primary responsibility of the administration to prevent injuries. This may mean the use of uniformed police. This must be prepared for by a precise and careful plan, prepared in advance between the chief administrators of the schools and the police. Every effort must be made to prevent overreaction, but bodily injury to innocent people *cannot be tolerated.* There is no question that extremist factions of many different groups are deliberately seeking physical confrontation. It *must* be prevented.
5. Planning ahead for trouble can no longer be considered an overreaction. The record shows that injuries and even death have resulted from poor planning and a lack of insight into the possibilities of extremism.

The worst possible course of action is to have substantial reforms granted only *after a show of violence.* This plays directly into the hands of fanatics. The reforms should be made *before* the violence. Prevention is always easier than cure.

Chapter 2 contains an abbreviated checklist developed from a specific manual prepared by an administrator who faced a protest march in 1969. It is not intended to be a definitive manual, but merely a set of guidelines involving the various elements of precaution required for a school district facing possible trouble. Your district and your school have unique characteristics which require tailor-made precautions. Work them out with the people who are closest to each situation, get them in writing, and have them in the hands of the people who will be on the firing line.

Riots are minor wars. Wars cannot be fought democratically. Authority and obedience are essential. Democracy returns when the emergency has ended.

The Deluge of Drugs

The frightening and frantic increase of drug abuse among our young, and, more recently, among the young of other nations, hardly needs documentation here. That it has happened at all is horrible; that it is a *youth* movement is terrifying.

Drug abuse, and notably the use of marijuana, has spread rapidly from urban ghettos to our suburbs and from our colleges down through the high schools into even our elementary schools. Questions need to be answered. Why do the young feel they need this dangerous form of escape? Escape from what? What can we do about it?

It is perhaps significant that they have rejected the major escape mechanism of some of their elders—alcohol. Drugs are *their* thing. Chalk up another rejection phenomenon of the generation gap, and in this case most especially of the credibility gap. We have told too many lies about drugs, especially marijuana. This is unfortunate since the truth is powerful enough. It is clear that we need to address ourselves, quickly and effectively to both horns of the dilemma—a removal of the need and a removal of the supply.

Part of the problem lies in the powerful attraction of a passing fad. Some youngsters today even pop harmless candies into their mouths in the hope that their peers will think they are indulging in "uppers" and "downers." This silly aspect of a serious problem will probably disappear when the kids become bored with it. The more serious aspects, however, must be dealt with vigorously. We must learn the truth and tell the truth about drugs. We must shift the emphasis from fear to insight. We must bust the pusher and help the addict. Everyone concerned with youngsters, and especially parents, must be taught about the problem and join the team effort to eliminate this monstrous blight.

Action

1. Stop using lies and half-truths in the battle against drugs. The truth is a powerful weapon. Learn the truth. Use it. Thirty to 40 years ago lies were told to the young about alcohol when the truth would have sufficed. The young discovered the lies. Alcohol education of that period was nearly a complete failure. If the young refuse to heed the lessons of history, at least the elders can.
2. Learn as much as you can about drugs. Some information is summarized in Chapter 3. A great deal more is needed. This information must be relayed effectively to teachers and parents in continuing drug education.
3. Youngsters, down to the first grade, must have regular, effective, and truthful drug education which will stress enlightenment.
4. Drug education for teachers and parents must break down the popular notion that drug abuse cannot affect *my* school, *my* child. Children and youth who use drugs come from *all* sections of society. Unless this obvious truth can be accepted, valuable time will be lost in the treatment of victims and the elimination of traffic in narcotics.
5. A working relationship must be established with the police which does not interfere with their basic job of arresting those involved in drug distribution. This must be done without interfering with the school's basic job of helping students. This is a tall order. It can only be accomplished through close and careful liaison between police and school officials.
6. Policies and regulations regarding drug abuse must be care-

fully prepared and widely distributed. Their preparation must involve police officials and should involve students as well as teachers, administrators, and parents.

7. One professional educator should have the chief responsibility for a continuing drug education program and should have the material and moral support of all concerned.
8. Alcohol and tobacco education should be included in the drug program since both of these are problems in many schools along with other drugs.

The role of the teacher must be stressed in drug education, especially that of the young teacher who may have a liberal attitude about drugs, especially marijuana. There is no excuse for any teachers to communicate permissiveness to young students about the use of any drugs. This is an inexcusable offense to be dealt with most severely. All teachers must be part of a team in this difficult battle for the health and well-being of our students.

The Payoff Is the Classroom

Our schools have been the targets of criticism since *Sputnik I*. Before that, they were targets of not so benign neglect. We who work in the schools have reacted in a normal defensive way by diverting some of the blame to others. Criticism and blame must now be minimized and replaced by accountability. Accountability begins in the classroom. Are students learning what they are supposed to learn? There is formidable evidence that they are not, especially in the cities.

Alternative ways to better learning are being proposed, blueprinted, and demonstrated by private industry with apparent success. Teacher organizations are accusing these efforts of being without truth and substance. In spite of minimal justification for these criticisms, it seems to me that the object is to improve learning by whatever means can be devised. If we can do a better job in the conventional classroom, let's get on with it.

Student complaints about schools are being heard throughout the land. Painfully similar threads run through these gripes. An image emerges of schools based upon fear and blind obedience to authority, a system that encourages student dishonesty and discourages creativity and joy in learning, a system that thrives on student failure.

The implied criticism of our courts in recent decisions extending to our students their basic rights and freedom of choice as citizens cannot be shrugged off lightly. We can easily point to improvements in our schools in recent years. Our best schools are very good indeed. But we must open our eyes to the fact that our total effort must be improved and that the improvement must be focused on what happens in the classroom.

Action

1. Every teacher should start to improve classroom climate by honestly examining his own *attitude*. This examination should go beyond his actions and words to his *subliminal communications* which cause "gut reactions." *Acceptance* of individual students as they are must come before an improvement of their values and aspirations.

2. The teacher must learn truly to *listen* to students and heed their reasonable complaints. Listening to students would include even lesson and unit planning, evaluation of student performance, and the whole professional arsenal heretofore reserved for professionals only. It is time to hear the consumer's voice in these matters.

3. Nothing really new is needed in the improvement of instruction. What is needed is more attention to what we already know. If every teacher *truly* heeded one piece of advice, enormous improvements would come to pass: *You have learned some rules for good teaching. Do not waive these rules. You can no longer get away with it.*

These things are, of course, easier to write into a book than to carry out in the classroom. It seems very clear that teaching will become more and more difficult in the years ahead. Why should this be cause for anxiety? As the substance of our profession improves, our results will improve. As our results improve, our rewards will improve—extrinsically and intrinsically. That's what accountability means.

A Democratic and Humanitarian Base for Discipline

Change is a primary ingredient in a democratic society. Change in our institutions reflects the changing needs of our people. The system of discipline in our schools must reflect the principles of that democratic society and must be flexible enough to provide for the changing needs of students. Eternal values need not be abandoned in this change. They should and can be strengthened by it.

The foundation of disciplinary procedures must be in law as it is written and interpreted at all levels. Our laws are constantly changing, as written and interpreted. We must follow these changes and respond to them in the schools. The shift in emphasis from *in loco parentis* and the stress on *due process of law* for students cannot possibly be interpreted as the abandonment of the value known as equal justice for all. It is, rather, *an extension of that value* to an area where the courts feel it has been denied.

The principle of "reasonable supervision" is still very much with us and must be maintained in the face of increasing demands by teachers to be relieved of "non-professional" duties. A revised system of discipline must be created which will take into account these changes, extending rights to students; the necessity of preserving reasonable supervision; the necessity of protecting the safety, health, and well-being of students; and which extends a humanitarian concept of law, order, and *justice* to the individual.

Action

Regulations, policies, and procedures must be based upon the following facts of life as school people face them in the seventies:

1. Students do not abandon their constitutional rights when they enter a school. Schools can no longer be guided by the right to do anything a reasonable parent would do.
2. American citizens have every right to advocate unpopular change. They may even organize to implement unpopular change. But they may not break the law in so doing.
3. Law-breaking must be referred to the proper law enforcement agencies.
4. Freedom of speech must be maintained, but there are now, and always have been, limitations on freedom of speech. This freedom does not extend to inciting to violence, interfering with the freedom of others–or the educational opportunities of others, or slandering another person.

Action Review

5. Underground newspapers usually begin because official publications are inadequate, dull, or too heavily censored. They usually fail quickly because of lack of sustained energy, funds, and writing talent. They should be subject to the same legal restraints as any conventional publication.
6. Compulsory ceremonies, such as the flag salute, are now on dubious legal grounds. There is great need for education of a positive nature, especially at lower levels, on the meaning of patriotic ceremonies.
7. Clothing or dress of students has been taken out of the control of the teachers and principals, except when it demonstrably interferes with education, health, or safety.
8. Schools still retain rights of suspension and expulsion under law, even when general poor behavior is cited as opposed to a single overt act, but due process must be followed. This does not necessarily include the right of legal representation when the possible punishment is minor.
9. Search and seizure must be handled with care and with a knowledge of the most recent judicial decisions.

Justice, Law, and Order

A primary concern, under law, of the school administration, is the safety, health, and well-being of all students. All teachers must share this concern for all students at all times.

School disciplinary procedures of the past have differed from our regular court procedures in at least one significant way. Because the consequences of rule-breaking in school are far less serious than those of law-breaking in adult society, our courts and schools exhibit opposing emphasis in respect to protecting the innocent. Our courts often err in the direction of *not* convicting the guilty in their zeal to protect the innocent. Our schools frequently punish the innocent in their zeal to prevent the guilty from going unpunished. Remember the silly practice of keeping an entire class after school because a teacher could not identify the noisy ones? This is the type of thing being challenged by our courts.

The discipline operation needs to be broadened considerably in the average school. It must reflect the fact that everyone should assume responsibility in this area. While justice is most important, it is also necessary to maintain law and order. We should never forget that fascism seized power in Germany and Italy when law and order broke down.

Action

1. Teachers should participate in a disciplinary council, both to recommend policies and to process minor referrals.
2. Counselors should be deeply involved in preventive discipline.
3. Instructional supervisors, such as department heads and grade-level chairmen, should be directly involved in disciplinary cases arising out of instructional and curricular deficiencies.
4. It may well be time to re-examine the more or less extinct student court and give it a new look and a new chance in a new age. We should not recreate the previous format, but seek a new design.
5. There should be regularly scheduled periodic discussions between small groups of students and teachers about discipline.
6. A precise plan of procedure should be available for working with local and state police, both in law enforcement and in education on such matters as narcotics and traffic safety.
7. All school personnel should be organized for varying emergencies so that everyone knows where he should be and what he should do under all conditions.

The Problem of Alienated Youth

Students with exceptional characteristics or defects have, in the past, been largely neglected in our public schools. This is part of the reason for the growth of our independent schools, particularly near the larger urban centers. In recent years, however, a great deal of new money and new effort have been expended on varying types of exceptionality. With this thrust in the area of varied learning disabilities and handicaps, we can look forward to an improvement in the mainstream of education, which will be relieved of a major portion of the responsibility for corrective instruction. In the meantime, we must note that far greater efforts must be made in the work with emotionally disturbed youngsters. And, perhaps, the most difficult problem of all remains as formidable as it has ever been—the problem of just plain "turned off" kids.

This student often has normal or better verbal potential, cannot be classified in any other category of exceptionality, operates academically at a marginal failing to a total loss level, and is generally eagerly awaiting his sixteenth birthday (or whatever the magic number is in his state) so that he can legally leave the prison that school has become for him.

At this point in his life, even kindness and personal attention are only temporary palliatives. A get-tough policy does not impress him at all. He has gone that route too often. His anger and frustration lead to anti-social behavior. Sooner or later he begins to interfere actively with the learning opportunities of other students. Something must be done.

Action

1. A school district with a large number of alienated youngsters must be doing *something* wrong. That something must be identified, acknowledged, and corrected. Quite often the problem is rooted in curriculum and instruction. Is this student being exposed to a watered-down college preparatory curriculum? Is the work too hard for him? Too easy? Quite often the latter is true.

2. The learning experiences of alienated students *must* be appropriate to the individual in terms of content relevancy, level of difficulty, rate of learning, and style of learning.

3. Every effort must be made to keep the student in the regular school program, but to provide him with appropriate instruction and necessary remedial assistance. If this fails, a *segregated* grouping is essential.

4. A segregated program must include: (a) a low pupil-teacher ratio, somewhere around one to ten; (b) exceptionally able teachers with special training and the support of a psychiatrist or psychologist; (c) good physical conditions with facilities for physical activities; (d) provision for close liaison with the home and the regular school to which the student may return—this would require a social worker if more than 20 students are enrolled; (e) provision for a partial return to regular school as soon as possible; (f) a strong emphasis on vocational guidance and, if at all possible, a work experience program under strong supervision.

Expensive? Of course it is. In a district carrying a per pupil cost of around $1000, this type of program would probably cost at least $2000 per student. If the program can redirect *half* of its students, it is well worth the money. Prisons cost around $6000 per inmate per year to operate. Chapter 7 describes some programs of this general type which seem to have experienced success with at least some of these alienated youngsters who have been neglected too long.

Human Relations Training

A powerful lubricant for the machinery of change has become increasingly evident in recent years. This phenomenon can be called *human relations training.* In its simplest and most effective form, it consists of a small group (a dozen or so) of people meeting in an unstructured and unthreatening atmosphere, for extended periods of time, under the guidance of a skilled leader who plays the role of one who is present to optimize the learning process.

The process must be separated from similar groupings created for *therapy*. This is education *about* human relations, not therapy. Emotionally unbalanced people may benefit from group therapy, but they do not belong in a human relations training group.

A good human relations program must be designed for emphasis in terms of a clearly stated major goal. This goal often is, but need not be, the minimizing of racial conflict. *It can be the improvement of school discipline.* It can be simply to reduce resistance of teachers to change. When it is conducted by the right people, human relations training can be amazingly effective. When conducted by poorly trained people, or charlatans, it can be downright dangerous.

Action

1. Begin with an understanding of what good human relations training can and cannot accomplish. It *can* counter prejudice with information, present to minority groups viable alternatives to violence, equip teachers to deal more effectively with increasingly militant students, and improve attitudes of many people to others. It *can* stimulate desirable change and help teachers to understand the role of emotions in teaching and learning. It *cannot* possibly help some people. It *cannot* accomplish miracles. It *cannot* correct deeply seated attitudes.

2. Take great care in selecting the right trainer. Begin by checking with administrators who have been involved in a program of this type and whose judgment can be trusted.
3. Write for information to the major sources listed in Chapter 8.
4. Prepare with the assistance of the staff a reasonable list of goals to be accomplished by the program. Then go over these with the chief trainer to be involved. A certain way to ensure failure is to insist upon unrealistic goals, particularly for a limited program.
5. Prepare carefully all personnel who are to be involved so that all possible fears and misinformation are eliminated. It is wise to enlist the assistance of the trainer in a face-to-face meeting with all who are to be involved, at which time complete information is made available about all facets of the program.
6. Encourage the participation of all people for whom the program is designed, but do not *insist* upon it.
7. Obtain a realistic assessment of what the program will cost, both in money and in time during which teachers will be released from classrooms. The release of a teacher from her regular class is a loss in instructional effectiveness whether or not a qualified substitute is provided. Principals must know this in advance and must be carefully briefed on the expected gains which will compensate for this loss.
8. Check out all possible sources of funding. Use the *Foundation Directory* cited in Chapter 8. Some human relations trainers are highly regarded by foundations and public officials responsible for various types of assistance to school districts.

A sound human relations program of the type described in Chapter 8 can do a great deal of good in the classroom. While it may not resolve deeply rooted racial tensions, it can prevent crises so that the school district can correct inadequacies and prepare itself for possible conflict. It is my opinion, regretfully stated, that tragic racial conflict lies ahead. The schools are very vulnerable and must face the cruel realities of the years to come. One way to approach this seemingly insoluble problem is to create a continuing program of human relations training.

Policies and Regulations

School disciplinary procedures are built on a foundation of philosophy and law. The law extends downward from the Supreme Court rulings to the local policies and regulations governing disciplinary practices. Recent years have seen a great emphasis on the *rights* of the individual student in our schools. Perhaps this emphasis has obscured the *responsibilities* of the individual, especially as they affect the rights of all. In any event, it must be made clear to everyone that no rights are absolute. Every right has limitations. The spelling out of these limitations must be found in the policies and regulations of the school district and the individual school.

Action

1. All policies and regulations should be reviewed in the light of recent court decisions and the increased militancy of students, teachers, and nearly every segment of the community.
2. Basic citizenship rights, including due process of law, *must* be extended to students in school policies and regulations.
3. The guideline of interference with the educative process must be clearly indicated in policies and regulations which circumscribe the actions of individual students.
4. Broad participation is essential to an orderly and sensible review of existing policies and regulations. This should include responsible and mature students.
5. All participants should be briefed by an attorney on recent court decisions concerning the operations of schools.
6. Guidelines should be developed along the lines cited in Chapter 9, to prepare policies and regulations.
7. Old policies and regulations which are in contradiction to current court rulings must be changed or eliminated, no matter how much the local citizenry may disapprove of the court actions. School administrators and elected school board members are charged with upholding *all* laws, not merely the ones they like. Bad laws and bad interpretations of law can be changed. Until they are changed, they must be obeyed.

Note: A good illustration of the rapid pace of change in interpretation of law is the proposed policy on the flag salute ceremony presented in Chapter 9. Approximately four months passed between the time that policy was presented and this writing. In that time, court rulings have been handed down which seem to make *any requirement* to participate in the flag salute ceremony unconstitutional. In April, 1971, a proposed law requiring the flag salute through the state of Massachusetts was returned to the Education Committee of the state legislature by the Governor on the grounds that it was probably unconstitutional. The Governor proposed, in amendment, that daily patriotic readings be substituted for the flag salute. In other words, it is possible that very recent policies may become as obsolete as the older ones. School boards and administrators must remain constantly aware of the rapidly shifting legal picture in America today.

Note: The policy cited on the *Constitutional Guaranties to Juveniles* will probably remain legal for some time to come, but the cited reference to *in loco parentis* as a basis for corporal punishment in Pennsylvania law will very likely be challenged and discarded.

8. The principle of foresight should be exercised in reference to policies and regulations on narcotics, even by districts which have not yet experienced the problem. The narcotics problem has appeared in very unlikely places in the past and will probably continue to do so in the future.

The writing of policies and regulations along with constant modifications thereof, has always been a difficult and time-consuming task in districts which place importance on these matters. Because of rapidly changing times, the task has become even more difficult today, but there is no easy solution. The work must be done, and it must be done well if we are to function efficiently and effectively.

Discipline and Better Arrangements for Learning

It has been well established that many problems of discipline proceed from a meaningless curriculum, poor teaching, and a school organizational pattern which dehumanizes the individual. Thus, one effective way to improve discipline is to improve instruction and school organization.

Schools are difficult to change. Resistance lurks everywhere. New patterns, even when put into effect, are hard to maintain.

But it seems very clear that substantial and lasting reforms must be made *and maintained* in our schools. New ideas are not really needed. What is required is the implementation of good and old ideas which have not been given a chance in many schools—ideas which have proven themselves effective in some schools for many years.

Action

1. New machinery for change must be designed—machinery that incorporates the best of what has been successful in the past, machinery that draws liberally from the resources of both private and public sectors of our society. America needs a united front for educational reform. One possible approach has been briefly outlined in Chapter 10. Perhaps it is far from perfect, but *something must happen soon.*
2. We must identify goals and order our priorities. Three of the most promising movements in education today are, in my opinion, the following: (a) the reorganization of curriculum content to make it relevant for *today's students;* (b) major movements into individualization of instruction and a change in the role of the teacher from that of a communicator to that of an organizer and prescriber of learning experiences on the basis of individual needs; (c) opportunities for continuous progress of students by elimination of the lock-step system of grades K-12.
3. We must master the technology of these three major movements and get moving on their implementation.

We have seen successes in American education through the use of many differing organizational patterns and many new artifacts, notably computers. In every instance, the success was not merely indicated by improved achievement scores, but also by a significant improvement in the tone of the entire school, in general morale, and in better discipline.

This is a book about discipline. What I have tried to say may possibly be reduced to two short sentences: Good discipline does not create good schools. Good schools create good discipline.

Index

A

Absenteeism, 45
Accountability, 69, 163
Action review, 176
Adolescence, problems of, 59
Adulthood, recognition of, 38
Alcohol education, 55, 181
Alienated youth, 115
American Association of School Administrators, 115
American Education, 157
Amphetamine, 63
Anarchy, 40
Apartheid, 28, 29
Appalachia, 159
Arrangements for learning, 191
Arrests in school, 148, 154
Atlanta Metropolitan Area, year around school in, 165
Attendance taking, 175
Attitude, change of in the young, 178
Attitude of young soldiers, 31
Authoritarianism, 89
Authority of professional employees over pupils, 150
Auxiliary administrative unit, 160

B

Backlash, 24
Bad laws, enforcement of, 190
Basic issues, common, 36
Behavior codes, 96
Berkeley University, 21, 22
Bennies, 63
Bethel, Maine, human relations training in, 128
Biblical season for ideas, 174
Bigart, Homer, 42
Bigotry, 131
Bill of Rights, 143
Biracial school, 29
Birmingham, John, 39
Birnbaum, Max, 132
Black Americans, militancy of, 20
Black studies, 28
Blue collar workers, 38
Board of School Directors of Bristol Township, Pa., 144
Bomb scare, 148
Bond, common among revolutionaries, 30
Bootleg alcohol, 54
Boston Herald Traveler, 60
Boston University Human Relations Laboratory, 135
Boycott of classes, 43
Braille, 119
Brainwashing, 131
Bristol Township, Pennsylvania, 133
  Opportunity School, 124
  police, 139
Britain, drug problem in, 53
Brittenweiser, Peter, 121
Brown, Frank, 163
Brutality and force, 24
Bucks County Courier Times, 138
Building security, 51
Bullhorns, 51
Buses for emergencies, 114
Buttons with slogans, 93

C

Califano, Joseph A., Jr., 53
Campus, open, 174
Canada, drug problem in, 53
Censorship of student views, 41
Ceremonies, compulsory, 185
Chain of command, emergency, 51

Index

Change coalition, 32
Channeling of power, 26
Checklist, emergency, 50
Chicago Ray School, 123
Chicago riots, 21
Chicanos, 178
City University of New York, 28
Civil Rights Act of 1964 (see Public Law 88-352, p. 134)
Civil Rights Movement, 28
Clerical training, 171
Climate, classroom, 74, 161, 163
Clothing and dress of students, 185
Coal regions of Pennsylvania, 134
College administrators, 28
Columbia University, 29
Command functions, 110
Communications, internal in emergency, 114
Communications, subliminal, 74
Communism, incipient, 38
Communist Party, American, 90
Complaints, student, 72, 182
Computers, 164
Confrontation, 41
Confrontation politics, 40
Constitutional rights, 96, 97
Consultants, 160
Consultation to teachers, 173
Continuous progress, 163
Co-opted by the Establishment, 26
Cop out of young generation, 31
Corporal punishment, 98
 Pennsylvania law on, 149
Correctional institutions, 117
Council Rock, Pa. School District, 50
Credibility gap, 41, 178
Criminal investigation in schools, 147
Criticism of schools by courts, 183
Cubans, 30
Curriculum:
 academic, 87
 reform of, 89
 use by teacher, 80
Cutting classes, 175
Cynicism of students, 38

D

Dangerous conditions:
 in emergency, 113
 potential, 113

Data cards, 41
Data processing, 163
Department heads, 104, 186
Dependency, psychological through use of marijuana, 59
Depression of the 30's, the, 26
Dextroamphetamine, 63
Differences, institutional, 36
Differentiated staffing, 173
Disciplinary council, 186
Discipline:
 democratic base for, 183
 policies affecting, 141
 policies and regulations for, 142
 preventive, 104
 principles of secondary school, 84
 problems connected with drugs, 61
Discipline/punishment, sample policy, 149
Disruption of school, 155
 sample policy, 156
Distributive education, 170
Dogs, police use of, 139
Downers (see Drugs, depressant)
Dress, battle, 47
Dropouts, 45, 116
Drug control policy, 151
Drugs:
 depressant, 64,
 stimulant, 63
Drug use, suspicion of, 152
Due process of law, 86, 102, 184

E

Educational Cabinet of the Bristol Township School District, 143
Education, outdoor, 67
Education USA, 86
Elfenbein, Dr. Morton H., 136
Enforcement of law, 107
Establishment, the, 19
Eternal values, 184
Evidence, interpretation of, 177
Experimentation, 158
Expulsion, 97
Extended school day, 166
Extended school year, 165
Extremism, 179

F

Falmouth Enterprise, 32
Family groups, 122

Index

Fascism, 186
Federal aid, 159
Felony, conviction of by use of marijuana, 58
Fifties, decade of, 20
First aid stations in emergency, 52
First Amendment of U.S. Constitution, 155
Flag, American, 94
Flag salute:
  compulsory, 94
  policy, 143
  Supreme Court ruling of 1954, 145
Fortas, Justice Abe, 83
Fosdick, Harry Emerson, 34
Foundation Directory, 133
Fourteenth Amendment to U.S. Constitution, 95, 143
Franklin, Ben, quotation on education, 78
Freedom of speech:
  limitations of, 184
  sample policy, 155
Fulton County, Georgia, 165

G

Generation gap, 27
Generation War Theory, the, 22
Germany, 186
Ghandi, Mahatma, 85, 90
Ghettos, 27
Goals and expectations, differences in, 37
Goals for improvement of education, ordering of, 181
Golden Rule, use of by teacher, 74
Goofballs, 64
Grade-level chairmen, 186
Graduate schools of education, aiding public schools, 159
Grass, change from weed, 56
Gratification, delayed, 38
Guidance counselors, 103
Guidelines for emergency, 113
Gut reactions, 74
Guys and Dolls, 55

H

Haircut, Afro, 29
Halfway houses, 66
Hallucinogens, 62
Handbook of School Letters, 140
Hard hats, 38
Hardware expertise, 173
Hardware, military, 31
Harlem, 37
Harvard Medical School, 67
Harvard University, 32
Harris, Louis, 32
Hebrew religion, early, 29
High school radicals, 178
High school students, 27
History, lessons of, 26
House Un-American Activities Committee, 25
Humanitarian and pragmatic bases for discipline, 88, 183
Human relations education, 127, 129
  cadre training in, 137
  goals of, 129
Human relations training:
  by-products of, 128
  charlatanism in, 132
  evaluation of, 136
  pitfalls in, 131
Hunt, Jane, 35

I

Ianni, Francis A. J., 70
Idealism, basic core of in youth movement, 177
Ideology of rebellion, 24, 25, 26
Identification cards, student, 112
Identity problem of black students, 29
Implementation of change, 158
Independent Learning Center, 123
Indian, American, 145
Indian reservations, 159
Individual improvement, 129
Individually prescribed instruction, 162
Industries, war-related, 37
Information center for emergency, 111
Informer, Irish, 30
In loco parentis, 86, 146, 149, 184
Instructional supervisors, 186
Intelligence quotient, enslavement by, 81
Intensive care unit, 120
Intergroup communications, 136

Involvement days, 48
IPI, 162
IRA, 30
Irish Revolution of 1916, 30
Iron Curtain countries, 19
Irrelevant, relevant synonym for, 27
Italy, 186

J

Jackson State College, 36
Jewish liberal students, 28
Job descriptions, 173
Judiciary, criticism of schools from, 73
Justice, law and order, 100–103
Juveniles, Constitutional rights of, 146
Juvenile rights, policy on, 146

K

Karam, Dr. Irving, 50
Karpas, Melvin, 83
Keniston, Kenneth, 17
Kent State University, 36, 42
King, Martin Luther, 90

L

Laboratory technicians, 173
Labor, American, 21, 36
La Guardia, Fiorello, 56
Larson, Knute, 83, 100, 140
Law and order, 88
Law as a base for discipline, 85
Law breaking, 184
Law firms, storefront, 31
Laws of Pennsylvania regarding flag salute, 144
Leadership training, 135
Learning climate, improvement of, 169
Learning disabilities, 186
Learning Institute of North Carolina, 120
Learning in the marrow bone, 121
Learning laboratories of private corporations, 71
Lewis, Dr. David C., 67
Liaison, in emergency, 111
Liberalism has Failed Theory, the, 22
Liberal movement of the 30's, 25
Life Magazine, 89
Log events in emergency, 52

LSD, 65
Lyons, Richard D., 54

M

McCarthy, Eugene, 21, 27
McGoldrick, James, 140
Maine, 159
Man vs. Machine Theory, the, 22
Marijuana, 55–60
  illegality of, 57
  Mexican, 59
Massachusetts flag law, 191
Mass arrests, 25
Mass media, influence of, 36
Medical attention for drug users, 152
Medical service in emergency, 112
Melting Pot Theory, the, 130
Merit rating, 173
Methamphetamine, 63
Mexican Americans, 30, 130, 145
Microcosm, high school as a, 39
Middle East, the, 24
Militancy, 49
Militancy and discipline, 178
Militarism, anti, 37
Minority groups, 130
Modular scheduling, 174
Moonlighting of teachers, 77
Moscow, 20
Motels, 32
Mutiny of soldiers in battle, 31

N

Narcotic drugs, 61–68
Narcotics problem, 53
National anthem, 145
National Association of Secondary School Principals, 35
National Institute of Mental Health, 60
National Magazine, 30
National Training Laboratories Institute, 133
National Training Laboratory, 128
Nation's Schools, 72
Nazi party, American, 90
Negotiations, 26
Nembutal, 64
New Left, the, 25
New Right, the, 25

Index

New York City, criticism of its schools, 73
New York City, heroin deaths in, 54
New York Times, 42
New York Times Magazine, 17
No change coalition, 32
Non-negotiable demands, 26
Non-segregated grouping, 125
Nurses' aide program, 171

O

Obligations, contractual of teacher, 75
O'Brien, Gregory, M., 136
Opium, 61
Outside Agitation Theory, 21

P

Packard automobile, 132
Parade Magazine, 106
Participatory Democracy Theory, the, 22
Pay stations in schools, 51
Pentagon, the, 21, 37
Peace Corps, the, 27
Permissiveness, 122
Personal appearance, 95
Personnel, organization for emergencies, 110
Personnel orientation, 50
Philadelphia Advancement School, 120
Philadelphia School District, 122
Philadelphia Sunday Bulletin, 106
Photography, use of in emergencies, 51
Pigs, 8
Pilgrims, the, 158
Pledge of Allegiance to the Flag (see Flag Salute, 145)
Polarization of black community, 29
Polarization of a campus, 25
Police and college riots, 25
Police liaison, 50
Police, use of, 47, 108
Policies and regulations for discipline (see discipline) 141
Positive change, agent of, 40
Possession of drugs on school property, suspicion of, 153
Pot, 56
Poverty as an evil, 25

Press liaison in emergency, 111
Prison costs, 188
Problem solving, 129
Procedures, quasi-legal, need for, 87
Professional growth, 174
Program elements for drug education, 66
Program Planning Budgeting System, 164
Progressive Labor, 25
Prohibition repeal, 55
PTA, 46, 179
Public housing, 32
Public information, 52
Public Law 88–352, 134
Puerto Ricans, 30
Punishment, 149
Pushers, 65
Putsch, the Munich Beerhall, 26, 110

Q

Quakers, the, 127

R

Racial violence, 129
Racism, 28
Radar equipment, school's, 45
Ramapo, New York, Regional High School, 106
Rate of learning, 162
Rationale for action, 177
"Real money," 159
Reconstructionist institutions, 177
Reconstructionists, 129
Reforms after violence, 180
Regents Exams, 79
Regulations:
  oppressive, 41
  policies affecting, 141
Renshaw, Mike, 138
Residential institutions, cost of, 162
Restaurant training, 171
Revenge, black, 30
Revolutions, equal but separate, 28
Revolutions in history, 27
Riots, 180
Rockefeller, John D., III, 19
Rogers, Carl, 128
Role of teacher as manager of learning experiences, 173

Rollins, Sidney, 163
Roosevelt, Eleanor, 139
R.O.T.C., 25
Rules for good teaching, waiving of, 183
Rumble, 42
Rumor clinic, 51

S

Sabbatical year for youth, 169
Sabotage, 44
Salaries, teachers, 77
Sale of drugs on school property, suspicion of, 153
Salvation Army, 124
Sampling techniques, 32
San Francisco State College, 24
Search of lockers in school, 148
Seconal, 64
Security, building, 51
Security in emergency, 51
Seizure of spaces, 43
Sensitivity training, 127
Shedd, Mark R., 121
Silberman, Charles E., 176
Silly putty syndrome, 158
Sixties, youth rebellion of, 24
Slow learners, 126
Slow-learning classes, 45
Slowdown, the, 43, 49
Slum housing, 23
Smoking area, 38
Social mobility, upward, 23
Songs of youth, 31
Special education training, 172
Specialists in the machinery of education, 173
Speed, 63
Sputnik I, 17, 69, 182
Staffing schools, 173
State Commissioner of Education, New York, 98
Stockade, revolt in Army, 31
Strike, student, 43
Stud spelling, 121
Student activism in high schools, 34
Student council, 45, 79, 179
Student court, 186
Student radicals, 20

Students for a Democratic Society, 21, 25, 36, 39
Style of learning, 162
Style setting, clothing and hair, 87
Supermarket training, 171
Supervision, reasonable, 88
Supreme Court of U.S., 141
Surgeon General of the U.S., 96
Suspension, 97
Symbolism, acts of, 93
Symptoms:
    depressant overdosage, 64
    hallucinogen overdosage, 63
    narcotic drugs, 62
    stimulant overdosage, 64

T

Teacher, role of in drug education, 68
Teachers, industrial arts, 51
Teachers, oversupply of, 174
Team leadership, 81
Telephone company, 51
Television:
    influence of, 21, 25
    instruction, 158
    teaching, consultation on, 173
Tenure laws, 41
Terminal education, assistant principal for, 172
Tetrahydrocannabinol, in marijuana, 57
T group (see training group), 128
Therapy, 188
Thomas, Dr. George, 166
Thomas, Norman, 20
Thoreau, Henry David, 85, 90
Tio Taco, 30
Tolerance is not enough, 74
Tourist centers and year around schools, 166
Traffic safety, 186
Training group, 128
Trenton, New Jersey, 124
Trip, LSD, 62
Trump, J. Lloyd, 35
Trust and truth, places of, 178
Turfs, 46
Turned off kids, 186

Index

U

Uncle Tom, 29
Underground press, 44, 91, 185
Unemployment, 41
Unrest, symptoms of, 45
U.S. Constitution, Fourteenth Amendment, see Fourteenth Amendment to U.S. Constitution, 95
U.S. District Court, 94
U.S. Supreme Court, 94
Uppers, (see drugs, stimulant, 63)

V

Vandalism, 44, 179
Vengeance, desire for, 29
Venn, Grant, 115
Viet Nam War, 19, 42
VISTA, 27, 159

Visitors' badges, 112

W

Walkie-talkie, 51
Wall Street riot, 42
Warrants for search, 148
Weathermen, the, 21
W.E.B. Dubois Clubs, 25
Wells, H.G., quotation on education, 79
Welfare clients, 26
Wille, Lois, 157
Woods Hole, 32
Work experience programs, 169
World War II, 26

Y

Young Socialist Alliance, 25
Youth Revolution 18